A Caribbean Accent to Shakespeare's Voice

Quotes, Paraphrases, and Burning Issues for Today's Audiences

Many Famous Passages Made Plain with Commentary, Caribbean Stories, and Biographical Recollections

Delpha Charles, Ph.D.

All rights reserved. No part of this book shall be reproduced or transmitted in any form or by any means, electronic, mechanical, magnetic, photographic including photocopying, recording or by any information storage and retrieval system, without prior written permission of the publisher. No patent liability is assumed with respect to the use of the information contained herein. Although every precaution has been taken in the preparation of this book, the publisher and author assume no responsibility for errors or omissions. Neither is any liability assumed for damages resulting from the use of the information contained herein.

Copyright © 2012 by Delpha Charles, Ph.D.

ISBN 978-0-7414-7215-1 Paperback
ISBN 978-0-7414-7216-8 Hardcover
ISBN 978-0-7414-7218-2 eBook
Library of Congress Control Number: 2011945500

Printed in the United States of America

This is a work of fiction. Names, characters, places, and incidents either are the product of the author's imagination or are used fictitiously. Any resemblance to actual events or locales or persons, living or dead, is entirely coincidental.

Published March 2012

INFINITY PUBLISHING
1094 New DeHaven Street, Suite 100
West Conshohocken, PA 19428-2713
Toll-free (877) BUY BOOK
Local Phone (610) 941-9999
Fax (610) 941-9959
Info@buybooksontheweb.com
www.buybooksontheweb.com

Dedication

For my beloved husband, Dr. John Charles, who has been my earthly inspiration and my best friend. Thank you for making me a happy resident of the "country" I call Amorland.

Acknowledgments

A FEW WORDS OF RECOGNITION AND APPRECIATION ---

To my husband for the many pleasurable moments we spent reciting and analyzing excerpts from some of Shakespeare's famous soliloquies, ones we had to memorize as students in Antigua, West Indies. You made my writing enjoyable rather than arduous.

To the loving memory of my mother, Mary Elizabeth Buntin; my father, John Philip Buntin; my sisters, Regina and Enid; my sisters-in-law: Amelia, Geraldine, and Kathleen; my nephew, Glenn; and my aunts: Mae, Sal, and Kit. They will not be forgotten.

To my sisters: Jean, Mariel, Liniel, Audrey, and Leona; my brother, Edson; my sister-in-law, Grace; my brother-in-law, David; my cousins (especially Iris—thanks for your encouragement and support); my nieces and nephews. I enjoyed our early years together.

To Todd Kelly for the technical support you provided throughout, particularly the times I was about to jettison my computer.

To the five ladies of *The View* who have contributed unwittingly to this project, it is incumbent upon me to say, thank you. I would be remiss if I did not acknowledge that as an avid "viewer" of *The View,* I decided to write this book one day while watching the show. First of all, I considered the fact that in her stella career, Barbara Walters, the consummate interviewer/journalist, has interviewed from princes to paupers—practically all notable personalities on planet earth. Naturally, were he alive today, I believe that William Shakespeare would feature prominently in the line up of "The Most Interesting People" interviewed by Barbara. But since he was not available for comments when she did her special eliciting opinions on "Heaven," I have included one or two statements in Chapter Three ("The Human Condition") that reveal some measure of Shakespeare's thinking on this subject. Also, I believe that, like all of Oprah's other guests, Shakespeare would have been pleased to sit on the famous couch and chat with the legendary "O".

Shakespeare's works are a cornucopia of "hot topics" identical or similar to many topics discussed on *The View*. I envisioned Shakespeare chatting with Barbara, Whoopi, Elisabeth, Sherri, and Joy; and I imagined myself in the audience waiting to ply the Great Bard of Stratford-on-Avon with questions. I also recognized that, coincidentally, in entitling her book *Audition,* Ms. Walters shares Shakespeare's perception of the world as a "stage" and men and women as mere "players." In her book's title, she has zeroed in brilliantly on the Sisyphus-like auditions that are sandwiched between all our lifetime "exits and entrances" (as Shakespeare puts it)—our constant strivings, our perennial endeavors.

Finally, to the Infinity Publishing Company I say thank you for allowing me the opportunity to be heard.

My Reasons for Writing This Book

Have you noticed that virtually every intelligent-sounding phrase of unknown origin is attributed to Shakespeare? Have you also noticed how a speaker or writer peaks the attention of an audience when he or she is able to quote a few pertinent lines from Shakespeare? And how often have you heard a quote from Shakespeare and didn't quite grasp its meaning? Or perhaps you are a politician or an orator who would like to borrow one or two lines from the great bard to enliven your communication and build your reservoir of ideas. And what about teachers and professors of English in high school and college who may need a Shakespearean "translation" to make the bard's immortal lines more meaningful for their students?

By the way, did you know that Shakespeare was the first to say, "Black is beautiful"? He said so in essence many centuries before this idea became a popular slogan in 1960's America (see Topic 19). Did you also know that it was Shakespeare who said, "All that glitters is not gold" and "Neither a borrower nor a lender be" (in *The Merchant of Venice* and *Hamlet* respectively)? In the academic world (from students to professors, from neophytes to literati), in the business world, in the political arena, in church sermons and other oratory, and even in amorous encounters, an apt quote here or there from Shakespeare is decorating utterances worldwide. I am, therefore, writing this book for all those (including me) who need a handy Shakespearean epigram, aphorism, or wise saying at the opportune time.

Gentlemen, who knows? When you summon up the courage to propose to your ladies, they may say "yes" more readily if you could impress them by whispering a line from Shakespeare in their ears. Indeed, I recognize that the so-called "strange" Shakespearean language often interferes with the acquisition of a suitable quote for a particular occasion. I write, therefore, to make Shakespeare a little more lucid, more accessible to general audiences, by paraphrasing or "translating" a number of his most famous passages. In my paraphrases, I have left the original words wherever the meaning is clear.

Throughout the years, many readers have also had a problem understanding the King James or Authorized Version of the Bible (1611). This difficulty with the seventeenth-century language has spawned many English translations or versions of the Bible. The following are just a few among over thirty contemporary English versions of the King James Bible: the Good News Translation (GNT), the New International Version (NIV), the American Standard Version (ASV), the English Standard Version (ESV), the Amplified Version (AV), and the New Revised Standard (NRS).

Well, Shakespeare and King James were contemporaries. They spoke and wrote the same language. It occurred to me, therefore, that the words of arguably the greatest, most renowned writer in literary history should also be translated, amplified, or reproduced in contemporary English.

No one is expected to tackle the daunting task of recasting all of Shakespeare's plays and sonnets into contemporary English. But I have found that paraphrasing a few famous excerpts was manageable and enjoyable. When I undertook this project, I had my students in mind. I recalled that though many of Shakespeare's words are the same as ours, many of my students typically refer to his language as Old English until I clear up the misconception, revealing that Shakespeare's language is Modern English, albeit NOT contemporary. Therein lies the "rub," since in the evolution of our language---and yes, language does evolve---some words have become obscure, some have undergone pejoration as well as other changes, and in some instances whole paradigms have been replaced. For example, notice the second person pronoun: seventeenth-century *thou, thee, thy, thine, ye* replaced by contemporary *you, your, yours.*

Little wonder, therefore, that a famous Hollywood actor made the following statement to Charles Gibson in an interview on ABC's *Good Morning America* (October 1990), as the two men discussed the actor's recent portrayal of Hamlet: "When I started studying Shakespeare, his language was like Greek to me," the actor confessed. " I think the key lies with the teacher to make Shakespeare accessible to students," he continued. That is what I have tried to do in this book: to remove the "Greekness" from selected segments of Shakespeare's writing. In spite of language barriers, many productions and reproductions of his works on the modern stage and in films attest to a certain intrigue Shakespeare holds for contemporary audiences.

My appreciation of Shakespeare's works has resulted in this project. Many of the themes or topics in his plays have triggered memories of my childhood in the Caribbean and my earlier years in the United States. An additional reason for writing this book, therefore, is to record anecdotes, recollections, my musings, and biographical incidents in the Introductions and Commentaries throughout the book. I enjoyed writing about my early island days, adding a touch of local color and a little narrative intrigue to my paraphrases.

In sum, Shakespeare's dramatic works have run the gamut of subject matter from love to war, from good to evil, from poverty to wealth; in other words, from birth to death and the hereafter. In this book, I have unearthed some of the pearls, the gems, the metaphors, the symbols, the universal themes and leitmotifs (in other words the "hot topics") that permeate his great works.

A Caribbean Accent to Shakespeare's Voice is unique because of its compelling blend of voices:
>voices of Shakespeare's characters
>voices of West Indian characters
>voices of Biblical characters
>the voice of the author paraphrasing, commenting, and providing the first detailed Shakespearean "translation" with a Caribbean flavor.

I have coordinated many Shakespearean themes in this book to produce a veritable symphony of voices and an intriguing sketchbook of relevant island stories with universal appeal. Hear Shakespeare call sleep the "chief nourisher" of life and watch a man sleepwalking in Antigua. Hear Shakespeare say love causes problems, and witness tragedy caused by love in Montserrat. Shakespeare denounces obsession with clothes; notice the negative consequence of a little girl's pride in her purple shoes. Observe King Hamlet's ghost walking and talking, and watch similar terrifying, supernatural occurrences unfold in Antigua and Montserrat. Picture a clear sky, a tropical sun, blue waters, and steel band music embellishing the scene, and you have a book that is arresting from beginning to end. Let us relax and enjoy Shakespeare, since we all have issues.

A Caribbean Accent to Shakespeare's Voice

The following is a list of the works of Shakespeare from which quotations or excerpts are paraphrased in this book---

PLAYS:

Hamlet
Cymbeline
Othello
Macbeth
King Lear
Pericles
Romeo and Juliet
Titus Andronicus
As You Like It
All's Well that Ends Well
The Comedy of Errors
The Midsummer Night's Dream
The Two Gentlemen of Verona
Love's Labor's Lost
2 *Henry IV*
Henry V
1 and 3 *Henry VI*

The Tempest
Richard II
Richard III
The Merry Wives of Windsor
The Merchant of Venice
Julius Caesar

POEMS:

Sonnet 18, Sonnet 27, Sonnet 28, Sonnet 116, Sonnet 147, *The Rape of Lucrece*

Contents

Acknowledgments i
My Reasons for Writing This Book iii
List of Works vii

1. **SLEEP: Quotes and Paraphrases**
   INTRODUCTION: A Vital New-Year Resolution—
           More Sleep 1
   The Innocent Sleep 6
   O Sleep, O Gentle Sleep 6
   Care Keeps His Watch 7
   Weary with Toil 8
   How Can I Then Return 8
   COMMENTARY: Your "Chief Nourisher" and Mine .. 9

2. **LOVE: Quotes and Paraphrases**
   INTRODUCTION 11
   Shall I Compare Thee to a Summer's Day? 11
   O Romeo, Romeo, Wherefore Art Thou Romeo? 15
   All the Other Passions 16
   Love Is a Smoke 17
   The Course of True Love 17
   Let Me Not to the Marriage of True Minds 18
   Oh, How This Spring of Love 18
   Love Is a Familiar; Love Is a Devil 19
   He after Honor Hunts, I after Love 20
   COMMENTARY: A Tragic Caribbean Love Story 21

3. **THE HUMAN CONDITION: DEATH AND OBLIVION OR HEAVEN AND ETERNITY AT LIFE'S END: Quotes and Paraphrases**
   INTRODUCTION...25
   For We Are Old...25
   Have You Not a Moist Eye...................................26
   We Are Such Stuff...27
   Tomorrow, and Tomorrow, and Tomorrow..................28
   As Flies to Wanton Boys.....................................28
   Of All My Lands..29
   For God's Sake, Let Us Sit..................................30
   All the World's a Stage......................................31
   Meeting in Heaven...33
   COMMENTARY: Childhood Fears of Death in Montserrat and Reassurance of Life In Heaven.................................33

4. **ADVERSITY: Quotes and Paraphrases**
   INTRODUCTION...39
   A Wretched Soul Bruised....................................42
   Sweet Are the Uses of Adversity..........................43
   Let Me Embrace Thee, Sour Adversity....................44
   COMMENTARY: Half an Island Paradise Is Better Than None.................................44

5. **STUDY---EDUCATION: Quotes and Paraphrases**
   INTRODUCTION...49
   What Is the End of Study?..................................54
   Study Is Like the Heaven's Glorious Sun................55
   My Years Are Young...56
   Some Food We Had...56

    COMMENTARY: The Cain Principle: Am I My
                           Students' Keeper? 57

6. **IS WAR A NECESSARY EVIL?: Quotes and Paraphrases**
    INTRODUCTION 75
    I See the Imminent Death...79
    O War, Thou Son of Hell 80
    Once More Unto the Breach 81
    Farewell the Plume'd Troop...83
    What Would You Have Me Do?..................................84
    COMMENTARY: The Paradox of Warfare:
                           Destroyer or Creator? 84

7. **RELIGION: Quotes and Paraphrases**
    INTRODUCTION 95
    The Advent Message Comes to Montserrat..................96
    Saluting Tabernacle on Its Fifteenth Anniversary 100
    The Coconut Grove SDA Church: Keep Striving! 102
    The Perrine SDA Church: Another Fledgling Soars....104
    Give Faith a Chance 105
    O God of Battles, Steel My Soldiers' Hearts!.............109
    And My Ending Is Despair 111
    The World Is Still Deceived with Ornament...............111
    COMMENTARY: A Tribute to New Carmel My
                           First Church.....................................112

8. **WORK ETHIC: Quotes and Paraphrases**
    INTRODUCTION 117
    Weary with Toil 118
    Therefore Doth Heaven Divide the State of Man 119

There Is No Ancient Gentlemen 121
What a Piece of Work Is Man! 122
COMMENTARY: The Catch of the Day in Salem 122

9. **RAPE: Quotes and Paraphrases**
   INTRODUCTION 125
   Lavinia, Wert Thou Thus Surprised 128
   But She Hath Lost a Dearer Thing than Life 129
   As the Poor Frighted Deer 129
   COMMENTARY: An Incident I'll Never Forget 130

10. **INCEST: Quotes and Paraphrases**
    INTRODUCTION 135
    Antiochus from Incest Lived Not Free 136
    Frailty, Thy Name Is Woman 137
    COMMENTARY: A Missing Father 138

11. **FRIENDSHIP: Quotes and Paraphrases**
    INTRODUCTION: A Salute To Antigua Girls'
       High School—Friendship In
       Brick And Mortar 139
    Since My Dear Soul Was Mistress 144
    Is All the Counsel that We Two Have Shared 144
    Antonio, I Am Married to a Wife 146
    COMMENTARY: Early Friendship—My Adolescent
       Family Life in Montserrat 146
    My Joyful Christmases in Montserrat 151

12. **DREAMS: Quotes and Paraphrases**
    INTRODUCTION 157
    Poor Wretches that Depend 158

Calpurnia Here, My Wife, Stays Me at Home 159
   COMMENTARY: My Knight and Amorland—
                a Dream Realized 160
Love Is a Country—Amorland: an Ode 164

13. SUICIDE: Quotes and Paraphrases
INTRODUCTION 167
To Be, or Not To Be—That Is the Question 169
Oh, that This Too Too Solid Flesh Would Melt 171
Then Is It Sin? 172
It Is Silliness To Live When To Live Is Torment 172
Even by the Rule of That Philosophy 173
Why, He That Cuts off Twenty Years 173
Here, Here Will I Remain 174
   COMMENTARY: A Caribbean Incident—a View
                from the Other Side of Suicide 175

14. CHILD ABUSE: A VOICE FOR THE INNOCENTS: Quotes and Paraphrases
INTRODUCTION 177
Ah, Clifford, Murder Not This Innocent Child 180
He Had Two Sons 182
   COMMENTARY: What Is Child Abuse? To Spank
                or Not to Spank; That Is the
                Question 183

15. MERCY VERSUS REVENGE: Quotes and Paraphrases
INTRODUCTION 189
Had I Thy Brethren Here 190
The Quality of Mercy Is Not Strained 193
Leave Her to Heaven 195

COMMENTARY: Mercy or Revenge? That Is the
                       Question..195

16. ASSASSINATION: Quotes and Paraphrases
   INTRODUCTION..197
   Romans, Countrymen, and Lovers! 198
   Friends, Romans, Countrymen, Lend Me Your Ears...202
   If It Were Done When 'Tis Done.................................217
   I Have Given Suck 219
   COMMENTARY: The Plurality of Assassination.....220

17. FATNESS/OBESITY: Quotes and Paraphrases
   INTRODUCTION..225
   If To Be Fat Be To Be Hated 226
   Let Me Have Men About Me That Are Fat.................227
   COMMENTARY: The Lean and Hungry Look 229

18. DRESS/CLOTHES: Quotes and Paraphrases
   INTRODUCTION..231
   There Can Be No Kernel in This Light Nut.................232
   Costly Thy Habit as Thy Purse Can Buy 233
   COMMENTARY: My Purple Shoes in Antigua—
                       Pride and Unfortunate
                       Consequences 234

19. RACIAL PREJUDICE: Quotes and Paraphrases
   INTRODUCTION..237
   He Hath Disgraced Me...241
   Stay, Murderous Villains! Will You Kill Your
   Brother?..242
   COMMENTARY: A Pricking and Bleeding in
                       New York 243

20. ALCOHOL ABUSE: Quotes and Paraphrases
   INTRODUCTION 249
   I Remember a Mass of Things, but Nothing
   Distinctly 252
   Though I Cannot Remember What I Did 252
   COMMENTARY: After Intoxication Comes
                        Transformation 253

21. PARENT/CHILD CONFLICT: Quotes and Paraphrases
   INTRODUCTION 255
   She Is Peevish, Sullen, Froward, Proud, Disobedient .. 257
   Hear, Nature, Hear, Dear Goddess, Hear! 258
   COMMENTARY: Sharper than a Serpent's Tooth
                        and More Deadly 259

22. THE SUPERNATURAL— SUPERSTITION—THE WORLD OF THE OCCULT: Quotes and Paraphrases
   INTRODUCTION 263
   Sir, Your Queen Must Overboard 267
   But It Is Doubtful Yet Whether Caesar Will Come
   Forth 268
   Ha! Who Comes Here? 269
   Angels and Ministers of Grace Defend Us! 270
   COMMENTARY: The Mysterious Hand and Bugs
                        from The Unknown 271

1. SLEEP

INTRODUCTION: A VITAL NEW-YEAR RESOLUTION—MORE SLEEP

Did you know that two-thirds of all Americans are sleep-deprived? Are you one of them? To be honest, I should have asked, Are you one of us? Yes, I am guilty. Do you sometimes fall asleep at work, at school, at church, on the bus, on the train—and perhaps even pass your stop? If so, don't be embarrassed. You are not alone. Nor should preachers be discouraged to discover that their sermons may have a sedative effect at times. Even St. Paul, that great preacher, lost one of the members of his audience to sleep (Acts 20: 9-12). It is my hope that St. Paul did not take it personally when Eutychus stopped listening to his sermon and succumbed to sleep. When Eutychus fell and died that day, he became one of the earliest victims of sleep deprivation. I am convinced that he did not mean to be disrespectful. After St. Paul restored him to life, Eutychus must have apologized profusely even as he said thank you. He was no different from those of us who struggle to keep our eyes open when a sermon is inordinately long.

I was born in the tiny British Caribbean island of Montserrat and grew up in the neighboring British island of Antigua which is more than three times the size of Montserrat and yet is, like Montserrat, a mere dot on the world map. During the early years, unlike the occupants of metropolitan American communities, the majority of the inhabitants of Antigua and Montserrat were early sleepers and, therefore, should have enjoyed many hours of restful sleep each night. Life is leisurely in these tropical islands, and yet there were several incidents involving sleep deprivation in both islands.

One day at church in Antigua, I noticed that Brother Henry Green had fallen asleep in a pew in front of mine. Suddenly, I heard a loud nasal roar and realized that he had begun to snore. Imagine my confusion when I recognized that his deep-throated, sonorous blast had reached a crescendo that would have silenced the preacher if someone did not shake this sleeper vigorously. Less than ten minutes later, to the consternation of all in the congregation, Brother Green got up from his seat and started walking towards the preacher. We watched bemused as he arrived at the preacher's side, a few feet before the first pew. He then walked past the preacher and disappeared into the vestry. One or two deacons rushed to overtake him and try to find out the reason for his strange behavior. To their surprise, they discovered that he was walking in his sleep. He later explained that he got up to go to the restroom. Actually, the restroom was located in the rear of the building.

Who among us cannot empathize with somnolent people like Eutychus and Brother Green? They were obviously sleep-deficient, and so are many of us. I have fallen asleep in my bathroom and even while standing erect in my kitchen. And how many of us fall asleep while we are praying? Isn't it wonderful that God never falls asleep while He is listening? Yes, there are times that sleep has immobilized us without warning. We succumb to sleep even in our cars. In a study published in a leading British journal in 2000, researchers in Australia and New Zealand emphasize the universality of sleep deprivation. They reveal the fact that inadequate sleep can lead to the same tragic results as alcohol impairment, causing sixteen to sixty percent of road accidents in various locations. Getting less than six hours sleep each night can affect coordination, reaction time, and judgment. The researchers found that motorists who were awake for seventeen to nineteen hours before they drove performed worse than those with a blood alcohol level of 0.8 percent which is more than the legal limit for drunk driving in the United States.

Without doubt, sleep is vital for optimal health and for our very survival on planet earth. Yet millions of us go without adequate sleep on a daily basis. Because I have been in the academic world for the better part of my life, I know what it means to burn the midnight oil. Our excellent, dedicated doctors, who are keepers of our health, work long, extended hours. Consequently, they also are often sleep deprived. As we pursue our goals and dreams, sleeplessness has become an epidemic, even a pandemic. Some people are taking supplements, as well as dangerous medication, and are literally dying to fall asleep. The recent death of one of Hollywood's most famous icons documents this fact. A television documentary recently disclosed that fifteen percent of adults in America admit that they have insomnia.. Indeed, we need to be reminded by Shakespeare of the enduring value of sleep.

Imagine that you have committed a serious crime, and you stand before a judge to be sentenced. You hear the judge's sentence: "You shall sleep no more!" You exhale, thinking—Is that it? My sentence could have been much worse! However, by day two of sleeplessness, your attitude will surely change.

Little wonder that in *Macbeth*, Shakespeare seems to be saying that the ultimate sentence anyone can pronounce on someone who has committed the most heinous crime is to deprive that person of sleep. Here's the situation: Macbeth, a nobleman in King Duncan's court, wants to be king; therefore, he conspires with Lady Macbeth (his wife) to murder the kind King Duncan while he is a guest at their castle. Macbeth's murder of the innocent King Duncan is bad enough, but the fact that he murders him while Duncan is asleep makes the act doubly abhorrent. Therefore, Shakespeare has the loud voice of Macbeth's conscience pass the most dreaded judgment on him. Over and over, Macbeth hears the harsh inner voice of vengeance condemning him to perennial sleeplessness: "Macbeth shall sleep no more" (*Macbeth* 2. 2. 43).

Consider this. What is the one thing we all MUST do whether young or old, rich or poor, short or tall, bond or free? Some may construe my question as faulty and insist that there are, in fact, two things that we humans must do: die and pay taxes. However, there are some people who are never required to pay taxes, and others may opt to go to jail instead of doing so. Obviously, there are a hundred-and-one things in our lives that we must do or suffer dire consequences if we don't. For example, eating is necessary to sustain life. However, an individual does not have to eat. He or she may decide to stop eating and embrace the consequences of starvation. Hence, no "mustness" there.

Therefore, let me pose the question again, seeking one word as an answer: What is the ONE thing we humans MUST do? No! The answer is NOT die! Shocked? Read on; I'll explain. Believe it or not, the answer is sleep. Granted, there are times that we try to resist sleep, but after a while, even involuntarily, our bodies surrender to the need for rest and slumber. Not even insomnia can keep sleep totally at bay.

From the cradle to the grave, we spend approximately a third of our lives asleep, and even the inevitable death is nothing but a sleep, as the literati often remind us: Why fear death, John Donne (1572-1631), an English poet, asserts: "One short sleep past, we wake eternally/And death shall be no more." Robert Frost (1874-1963), an American poet, also identifies death as a sleep. Like him, we have "promises to keep,/And miles to go before [we] sleep."

Here is one additional fascinating thought to drive home the fact that sleeping, not dying, is the one thing that all humans must do. Let me shock you again by declaring that not all mortals will die. Those of us who believe in the Bible will recall that the prophet Elijah (who lived many years ago) was one of the people who never experienced death but was, instead, translated—taken straight to heaven in a glorious chariot. What's more, we also learn in the Bible that, at the end of our mortal existence on this earth, many people will never die but will be translated as Elijah was. However, Elijah and all other translated mortals spent a significant part of their lives sleeping. Therefore, the ONE thing ALL mortals MUST do is sleep.

We cannot over-emphasize the importance of sleep. When the first "surgery" was performed in the Garden of Eden, even there the all-important sleep was instrumental: "And the Lord God caused a deep sleep to fall upon Adam, and he slept; and he took one of his ribs, and closed up the flesh instead thereof" (*Genesis 2:21*). Since then, how blessed we are to have our anesthesiologists who mercifully put us to sleep while our surgeons perform miracles and nothing less.

It is not surprising, therefore, that Shakespeare used so many words and such interesting imagery to emphasize the fact that sleep is the fountainhead of our humanness—a sine qua non for us, mortals.

The Innocent Sleep

-------the innocent sleep,
Sleep that knits up the raveled sleave of care,
The death of each day's life, sore labor's bath,
Balm of hurt minds, great nature's second course,
Chief nourisher in life's feast--------
(Macbeth 2. 2. 36-39)

***NOTE:** In profiling sleep in the above lines, Shakespeare uses personification and metaphor adroitly to present sleep as the main keeper of our existence.

PARAPHRASE

Sleep bestows innocence on the sleeper. In other words, an individual is free from guile as he or she sleeps. As thread restores a shredded garment, so sleep restores vitality to a care-worn frame. It kills or puts an end to the hectic activities crammed into each day. Sleep provides the soothing effect of water on dry, parched, work-weary bodies. It soothes and anoints troubled minds. It recharges the energy supply in our bodies, being nature's "second course" or second wind. If life were to be compared with a banquet, sleep would be the major course—the "chief nourisher."

O Sleep, O Gentle Sleep

O sleep, O gentle sleep,
Nature's soft nurse, how have I frighted thee,
That thou no more wilt weigh my eyelids down
And steep my senses in forgetfulness?
(2 *Henry* IV 3. 1. 5-8)

***NOTE:** Once more, we see the skillful use of personification as well as apostrophe to portray the restorative effect of sleep. Each night, we are revitalized—healed by "Nature's soft nurse." In many other passages, Shakespeare also uses personification to convey his ideas just as dramatically and with great clarity.

PARAPHRASE

Oh kind, gracious Sleep, you are a loving care-giver provided by Mother Nature. But to what extent have I frightened you that you will no longer make my eyelids heavy and saturate or drown my consciousness in peaceful slumber?

Care Keeps His Watch

Care keeps his watch in every old man's eye,
And where care lodges, sleep will never lie;
But where unbruised youth with unstuffed brain
Doth couch his limbs, there golden sleep doth reign.
(*Romeo and Juliet* 2. 3. 35-38)

PARAPHRASE

Worry or anxiety is a constant in the minds of the aged or mature, and a stress-filled mind does not allow the calming effect of sleep. But innocent, carefree youthful minds, uncluttered and unaffected by the cares of this life are subject to the powerful, soothing effects of that precious phenomenon known as sleep.

Weary with Toil

Weary with toil, I haste me to my bed,
The dear repose for limbs with travel tired.
But then begins a journey in my head,
To work my mind, when body's work's expired.
(Sonnet 27. 1-4)

PARAPHRASE

Tired after working, I hurry to my bed to rest my weary body. But sleep eludes me, and my mind begins to wander. When my physical labor is over, my thoughts keep me awake.

How Can I Then Return

How can I then return in happy plight,
That am debarred the benefit of rest?
When day's oppression is not eased by night,
But day by night, and night by day, oppressed?
(Sonnet 28. 1-4)

PARAPHRASE

How can I show up (reappear) in good condition when I am deprived of the advantages of rest (sleep)—when night does not bring relief from the trials of the day, but instead days are clouded by worry, and nights are oppressive because of lack of sleep?

COMMENTARY: Your "Chief Nourisher" and Mine

History does repeat itself. Once more, we witness the contest for occupancy of the White House. I wrote the following discourse years ago when I began writing this book. Naturally, as I watched the events unfold, I wrote in the present tense. I have decided to keep the present tense and ask my readers to travel back with me mentally, as we review the scenes together exactly as I described them more than three years ago. Let us pretend, for the next few minutes, that we have no knowledge of the outcome.

It is January 2008. History is being made even as I write. For the first time, among the candidates making a serious bid for the presidency of the United States are a woman, an African-American, and an Hispanic. An air of excitement blankets the campaign trail. As the candidates jostle one another, they throw many subtle and not so subtle missives at the opposing chariots lunging forward towards the prize. Meanwhile, we the spectators look on mesmerized, wondering how many bodies would be trampled by the time the dust clears. And, yes, all the while we find ourselves wishing, hoping, that a Ben Huresque champion would rise up and separate himself—herself—from the cluster and ride in triumph to the finish line amid our cheers and applause.

By the time this book is published, America will have her forty-fourth president who will usher in, we hope, the best of times, not the worst of times. From the sidelines, we watch the candidates as they shake hands, hug and kiss supporters, wave to the crowds, laugh, and perhaps even cry. However, what strikes us most poignantly is how seriously sleep-deprived they must be. As they make their marathon campaigning treks across America, sleep is possibly the most precious and most scarce commodity, even in greater demand than campaign funds. Undoubtedly, the candidates could use the "healing balm" of Sleep—that "foster nurse" that "knits up the raveled sleave" of our existence, as Shakespeare so aptly puts it. And so could we. Insomnia is a ubiquitous plague, that resides among us, at whom we regularly throw millions of dollars in sleep-inducing pills and potions. So many of us go about our daily affairs with minimal sleep. College students as well as professors, doctors, lawyers, business men and women, millions in varied walks of life move about, relying on a coffee-induced adrenalin to get through each day. We overlook the fact that sleep enables the body to repair itself and helps to fortify the immune system. To many, the recommended eight-hour sleep—even seven-hour—remains an unachievable luxury. We read of the havoc wreaked by drunk drivers—driving-while-intoxicated (DWI) drivers we call them. But what about sleep-deprived drivers? DWSD drivers I call them—**driving while sleep-deprived.** They are, we are, just as dangerous. Yes, I am guilty.

    I can recall a few occasions while on my way home from work, I would suddenly awake to the realization that several cars in my rear were waiting for me to move. In my confusion, I would look ahead to see a pair of large, green, piercing "eyes" staring at me accusingly, just as an impatient motorist would urge me on with a blast of his or her horn, seconds before green changed to red. I would then hasten home as fast as I could to make up for inadequate sleep. Shakespeare reminds us that sleep is our "chief nourisher" that reconnects the frayed pieces of our daily routine. So, starting today, we can all resolve to get a little more of "great Nature's second course"—the all-important Sleep.

2. LOVE

INTRODUCTION

Shall I compare thee to a summer's day?
Thou art more lovely and more temperate.
Rough winds do shake the darling buds of May,
And summer's lease hath all too short a date.
Sometime too hot the eye of heaven shines,
And often is his gold complexion dimmed.
And every fair from fair sometime declines,
By chance or nature's changing course untrimmed.
But thy eternal summer shall not fade,
Nor lose possession of that fair thou owest,
Nor shall Death brag thou wander'st in his shade
When in eternal lines to time thou grow'st.
So long as men can breathe, or eyes can see,
So long lives this, and this gives life to thee.
(Sonnet 18)

PARAPHRASE

In his Eighteenth Sonnet, Shakespeare (or the persona) asks the object of his affection rhetorically: Would it be reasonable to compare you to a day in summer? That would be pointless, because you are more delightful and agreeable. Not even the spring beauty of the month of May is comparable to your mildness and your charm because rough weather can occur in May (and destroy lovely flowers), but you are always temperate (or pleasant). And you excel the pleasurable days of summer because those days are too transient and unpredictable. On some summer days, the sun is scorching while at other times, quite often, the temperature is too cool because the sun's heat is diminished. And anything or anyone that is beautiful must lose his or her beauty eventually either fortuitously (by accident or chance) or because Nature—time—must run its course and take its toll. However, your natural, pristine radiance will not wane. Nor will you lose the loveliness you possess. In fact, Death will not be able to boast that he has claimed you as one of his victims. After I have immortalized you in this poem, you will be preserved to perpetuity. As long as there is life on this earth, you will live forever in this sonnet.

Unfortunately, unlike the picture of beatitude painted in Sonnet 18, love is often a turbulent experience. In Sonnet 147, the persona asserts that his love is comparable to an all-consuming, destructive fever. Many passionate lovers would agree: "My love is as a fever, longing still/For that which longer nurseth the disease,/Feeding on that which doth preserve the ill,/The uncertain sickly appetite to please" (lines 1-4). The speaker is declaring that his love is like a fever that continually demands the very thing that prolongs the effects of the disease, consuming only what makes the sickness more deadly. Some may argue that this second picture is a more accurate profile of love. In any case, regardless of the form love takes, we are all its victims. The word "victims" triggers the thought that love can sometimes turn dark, venomous, deadly, selfish, and vindictive. Too often we witness the "if-I-can't-have-you-no-one-else-can" mentality in lovers. Too often the headline news announces yet another murder/suicide—an action that seems to indicate that someone decided that death with a lover is better than life without the one loved. How sad! One wonders if this outcome is caused by psychopathic thinking. Only lunatics react in this way, we conclude. True love, real love, is not a destructive force, we argue. Sane people do not do insane things in the name of love, we insist. And yet, as we look back at our lives and those of others around us, we marvel at the disturbing things we see people do each day, all in the name of love.

For example, the world seemed to pause in stunned silence on that bleak day in 1936 when the debonair King Edward VIII gave up the great throne of England, driven by the overpowering love he had for the "forbidden" Wallace Simpson. His farewell address might have been labeled "a hopeless surrender to love." He confessed to the devastated English nation: "I have found it impossible to carry the heavy burden of responsibility and to discharge my duties as King as I would wish to do without the help and support of the woman I love." His abdication came after a period of tortured indecision. His action gives credence to the statement of Joseph Addison (1672—1719):

> Mysterious love, uncertain treasure,
> Hast thou more of pain or pleasure!
> Endless torments dwell about thee:
> Yet who would live, and live without thee!

How many of us could say we have gone through the better part of our lives unscathed by love? Very few, if any. To a large extent, we are all either beneficiaries or victims of love. We can therefore endorse a statement made by

Benjamin Disraeli (1804—1881): "We are all born for love. . . . It is the principle of existence and its only end."

Let's consider the fact that Shakespeare courted and married Anne Hathaway in 1582; they had three children, the first of whom—a daughter—was born in 1583; his only son died in1596; his life's work comprises many poems and plays depicting the delights and misfortunes of love. These facts suggest that, like the rest of us, Shakespeare must have had to grapple with and overcome the crucibles of love and emerge either a beneficiary or a victim.

So what is this thing called love? Who can define it? In 1184, Andreas Capellanus, an English courtier, embraced an assignment to write what may be deemed a primer for courtship. He titled his book *The Art of Courtly Love.* Courtly love was an ideal that flourished in medieval times at the courts of the European nobility. This ideal was expressed in the lyric poems of the troubadours (medieval poets and minstrels in southern France) as well as in romances based on the Arthurian legend.

Queen Eleanor of Aquitaine brought courtly love from Aquitaine first to the court of France and later to England. Her daughter Marie, Countess of Champagne, is said to be the one who assigned Capellanus the project to document the rules of courtly love. Here are some of these rules:

> The lady was to be worshiped from afar by her adoring gentleman admirer (her knight), not her husband.
>
> She had to appear disinterested and even fain rejection of his admiration.
>
> The love was pure, often not consummated.
>
> The gentlemen often did admirable deeds of chivalry to win the lady's heart. I can think of one such

example: Sir Walter Raliegh (1552-1618) is said to have laid his luxurious, expensive cloak over a puddle so that Queen Elizabeth I could walk without getting her feet dirty. And what about the chivalry that characterized Sir Lancelot and the other knights at the medieval court of King Arthur?

Our contemporary world has often declared courtly love and chivalry dead, though there are remnants here and there. Actually, we seem to be putting forth a collective effort to define love. What is it really? In my childhood in the Caribbean, I used to hear adults singing a little song with a simple message: "Love is a feeling that you feel when you're feeling a feeling you've never felt before." How true! Love is, indeed, a powerful feeling. It is the most universal of emotions, and yet it is a paradox: it causes joy but also pain; it causes laughter but also tears; it causes lack of appetite but also overeating; it causes lack of sleep but also sound sleep and sweet dreams. It makes us lose control and do strange things. In his sonnets, Shakespeare calls love a "madness," a "choking gall," and a "fever," yet he deems it a "preserving sweet." Can we call it anything different?

O Romeo, Romeo, Wherefore Art Thou Romeo?

O Romeo, Romeo, wherefore art thou Romeo?
Deny thy father and refuse thy name,
Or, if thou wilt not, be but sworn my love
And I'll no longer be a Capulet.
....
'Tis but thy name that is my enemy.
Thou art thyself, though not a Montague.
What's Montague? It is nor hand, nor foot,
Nor arm, nor face, nor any other part
Belonging to a man. Oh, be some other name!
What's in a name? That which we call a rose

By any other name would smell as sweet.
(*Romeo and Juliet* 2. 2. 33-44)

PARAPHRASE

Oh Romeo, Romeo, why are you called Romeo? Do not acknowledge your father and do not accept your name (i.e. change it). If you are unwilling to do this, then just promise to be my love (confess your love for me), and I will not be a Capulet any longer. It is only your name that stands between us (i.e. it is my only obstacle). If you were not a Montague, you would still be yourself intrinsically. What is so important about the name Montague? It is neither hand, nor foot, nor arm, nor face, nor any other part of a man's body. Oh, please take some other name! What's so important about a name anyway? If the flower which we call a rose were given a different name, it would have the identical sweet smell.

All the Other Passions

[A]ll the other passions fleet to air,
As doubtful thoughts, and rash-embraced despair,
And shuddering fear, and green-eyed jealousy!
O love, be moderate, allay thy ecstasy,
In measure rain thy joy, scant this excess!
I feel too much thy blessing. Make it less,
For fear I surfeit!
(*Merchant of Venice* 3. 2. 108-114)

PARAPHRASE

All other emotions such as doubt, sudden despair, fear, and jealousy lose potency in the presence of love. Love, be gentle! (i.e. Have pity on me.) Decrease your ecstasy or delight. Pour out your gratification more sparingly or temperately. Decrease this excessive delight. I am feeling too much happiness. Lessen the bliss I am experiencing, for if you do not, I might explode from too much pleasure!

Love Is a Smoke

Love is a smoke raised with the fume of sighs;
Being purged, a fire sparkling in lovers' eyes;
Being vexed, a sea nourished with lovers' tears;
What is it else? A madness most discreet,
A choking gall and a preserving sweet.
(*Romeo and Juliet* 1. 1. 196-200)

PARAPHRASE

Love is vapor or steam rising from passionate sighs or moans. In its purest form, it is a brilliant flame in the eyes of those who are in love. When love is thwarted or frustrated, the result is that the lovers' tears could fill an ocean. What else can be said about love? (In what other way can it be labeled?) It is most prudent lunacy. It is suffocating and bitter. And yet, it is an enduring delight.

The Course of True Love

Aye me! for aught that I could ever read,
Could ever hear by tale or history,
The course of true love never did run smooth. . . .
(*A Midsummer Night's Dream* 1. 1. 132-34)

PARAPHRASE

Dear me! In spite of anything I could ever read or ever hear in any fictitious or factual story, in reality true love was never given or received without some complication.

Let Me Not to the Marriage of True Minds

Let me not to the marriage of true minds
Admit impediments. Love is not love
Which alters when it alteration finds,
Or bends with the remover to remove.
Oh no! It is an ever-fixèd mark
That looks on tempests and is never shaken.
It is the star to every wandering bark. . . .
(Sonnet 116. 1-7)

PARAPHRASE

I will not allow problems or obstacles (impediments) to interfere with the sincere bonding of minds and hearts. True, real, or bona fide love does not change even though it is no longer reciprocated. Nor does it falter or disappear even though it is not returned. Oh no! True love is unswerving, steadfast, and enduring. It stands firm and unshaken in the fiercest storms. It is the night star, the lighthouse, the beacon to every ship that has drifted off course.

Oh, How This Spring of Love

Oh, how this spring of love resembleth
The uncertain glory of an April day,
Which now shows all the beauty of the sun,
And by and by a cloud takes all away!

(*The Two Gentlemen of Verona* 1. 3. 84-87)

PARAPHRASE

Young love or newly engendered love has all the freshness, splendor, and spontaneity of an unchartered spring day. It reflects all the brilliance and radiance of the sun. However, eventually, a mist passes over this scene and destroys it. In other words, love fades after a while.

Love Is a Familiar; Love Is a Devil

Love is a familiar; Love is a devil. There is no evil angel but Love. Yet was Samson so tempted, and he had an excellent strength; yet was Solomon so seduced, and he had a very good wit. Cupid's butt shaft is too hard for Hercules' club, and therefore too much odds for a Spaniard's rapier. . . The passado he respects not, the duello he regards not. His disgrace is to be called boy, but his glory is to subdue men. Adieu, valor! Rust, rapier! Be still, drum! For your manager is in love—yea, he loveth. Assist me, some extemporal god of rhyme, for I am sure I shall turn sonneteer. Devise, wit; write, pen; for I am for whole volumes in folio.
(*Love's Labor's Lost* 1. 2. 177-91)

PARAPHRASE

Love is a well-known phenomenon (a familiar spirit). It is a demon. There is no other emotion as evil or as treacherous. Yet, Samson allowed himself to be smitten by love, though he had incomparable strength. Solomon also allowed himself to fall prey to love, though he was the wisest man alive. Since the mighty Hercules has no defense against Cupid's darts, it is obvious that the sword of a Spanish warrior is useless. Love is no respecter of persons. The thrust of a sword in fencing or dueling does not deter Love. Those who portray Cupid as a boy have underestimated him, for he conquers men. Courage be gone! Sword rust in your sheathe! Be quiet, drum! Because the person who controls you is also vulnerable; he is in love. I invoke any god who inspires spontaneous poetry, for I feel that I am about to write sonnets to my love. Wit, stand by me! Give me ideas. Pen, write well! For I am about to write large, folio-sized volumes of poetry.

He after Honor Hunts, I after Love

He after honor hunts, I after love.
He leaves his friends to dignify them more;
I leave myself, my friends, and all, for love.
Thou, Julia, thou hast metamorphosed me,
Made me neglect my studies, lose my time,
War with good counsel, set the world at naught,
Made wit with musing weak, heart sick with thought.
(*The Two Gentlemen of Verona* 1. 1. 63-69)

PARAPHRASE

He chases honor; I chase after love. He leaves his friends to bring honor to them. I neglect myself, my friends, and all else for love. Julia, you have transformed me—made me forsake my studies, waste my time, ignore good advice and resist advisors. I place little or no value on all else in this world. I even made a weak effort to be witty; but all the while, I was sick at heart and preoccupied with thoughts of love for you.

COMMENTARY: A Tragic Caribbean Love Story

When a famous Hollywood actor jumped on Oprah's couch several years ago while discussing his love life, did he explode from too much pleasure, as Shakespeare puts it? Perhaps! An old proverb of unknown origin describes love as "a wildly misunderstood although highly desirable malfunction of the heart which weakens the brain, causes eyes to sparkle, cheeks to glow, and blood pressure to rise." And that is when love is reciprocated. Imagine when it's not. The ancient Greeks used several words to convey the idea of love, among them agape, philos, and eros.

Whether the spiritual, idealized agape, or the dispassionate, Platonic philos (filial), or the passionate love between lovers (eros), love is a powerful driving force, as Shakespeare reminds us. Too often we find ourselves torn in giving our allegiance to our spouses or lovers, while our relatives demand equal (sometimes greater) allegiance. An incident that occurred many years ago in the Caribbean illustrates a dilemma that resulted from the clash between filial (brother/sister) love and erotic love.

The day opened bright and refreshing in the beautiful island of Montserrat over sixty years ago. A blaze of excitement ignited and engulfed the young people in the large, exotic village of Salem. The long-awaited day for the exhilarating cruise around the island had finally arrived. The young people could hardly contain themselves because in a few short hours, they would be aboard a large boat with their boyfriends, girlfriends, lovers, and best friends. The boat arrived in the harbor at dawn. It rested on the crystal blue water waiting for its jubilant, euphoric young passengers to fill its interior.

At around ten o'clock in the morning, the boat pulled out of the harbor amid deafening applause from its occupants who ranged in age from sixteen or seventeen to the twenties. They waved goodbye to their fathers, mothers, and older relatives who were pleased to return home and let the young people enjoy their scenic cruise. Lively, rousing steelband music filled the air on the boat. The young people moved and grooved to the resonant strains of several popular calypsos—among them "Island in the Sun"—as they consumed mounds of rice and peas, curried meats, puddings, and gallons of ginger beer and sodas. Laughter was spontaneous, giggles abundant, and all that youth epitomizes defined the atmosphere on that boat.

Unfortunately, after approximately two hours, the sky suddenly turned dark grey. In less than no time, a violent storm developed. Mountainous waves enveloped the boat and tossed it around violently for a while. Each time the distressed boat leaned to one side, the terrified young people rushed instinctively to the other side. Eventually, the boat capsized.

At around five o'clock in the afternoon, a time when the mothers of Salem were fixing dinner and waiting for their youngsters to return home, a menacing scream pierced the stillness of the village. Loud moans, wails, and shrill cries violated the peaceful life in Salem as the mothers, fathers, sisters, brothers, and all the extended family members in this closely-knitted community gathered to come to grips with the heart-wrenching news that most of the happy young passengers on the boat had drowned.

This was the blackest day in the history of Salem. Even the lush vegetation, that is characteristic of the island, seemed to droop in sympathy that day. Many mothers thrashed around on the ground, wailing and bawling.

Suddenly, all eyes were on Mrs. Sarah Brown. She had collapsed, sprawled on her back, with her arms flailing and legs kicking. Her son Tom Brown was one of the few fortunate survivors who had swum to shore after the boat sank. But now, instead of embracing her son, Mrs. Brown was pushing him away and striking him and screaming at him: "Where is she! Where is she! How dare you! How could you! Where's my child? Me warn me chile!" She mourned pitifully. Those who managed to penetrate the crowd that had gathered around Mrs. Brown discovered that Tom Brown had saved his girlfriend, but his sister had drowned. No one knew the circumstance that produced this sad outcome. Tom was as devastated as the rest of Salem.

To this day, no one knows whether he deliberately chose his girlfriend over his sister. Perhaps Tom himself was not sure. It is quite possible that he simply grabbed the one person next to him, as he desperately tried to stay afloat. But in her grief-stricken condition, Mrs. Brown envisioned the two girls floundering in the ocean while Tom consciously and methodically reached for his girlfriend instead of his little sister. Mrs. Brown was inconsolable. It is said that she did not forgive her son until the day she died. Fortunately, many of us rely on agape love—God's healing love—to help us survive tragedies such as this one.

3. THE HUMAN CONDITION: DEATH AND OBLIVION OR HEAVEN AND ETERNITY AT LIFE'S END

INTRODUCTION

For We Are Old

For we are old, and on our quick'st decrees
The inaudible and noiseless foot of Time
Steals ere we can effect them.
(*All's Well that Ends Well* 5. 3. 40-42)

Who among us is not afraid or atleast reluctant to grow old? How many wouldn't give anything to stay the hand or the "noiseless foot of Time," as Shakespeare puts it?

Today, creams, potions, nips, tucks, lifts, and makeovers are more popular than ever, as we try to stave off old age. In the above quotation, Shakespeare reminds us that Time stalks us relentlessly in "inaudible and noiseless" steps, and before we know it, in spite of our effort to stay ahead, Time overtakes us and steals our youth. How true!

Shakespeare presents another disquieting reminder of our humanity and mortality in the following quotation:

Have You Not a Moist Eye

Have you not a moist eye? A dry hand? A yellow cheek? A white beard? A decreasing leg? An increasing belly? Is not your voice broken? Your wind short? Your chin double? Your wit single? And every part about you blasted with antiquity?
(2 *Henry IV* 1. 2. 203-07)

PARAPHRASE

Isn't your eye moist? Isn't your hand withered, dry? Isn't your cheek yellow, faded, and your beard grey? Aren't your footsteps much slower than they once were? Isn't your belly or paunch growing bigger and bigger? Isn't your voice weak? Aren't you often short of breath? Don't you have a double chin? Isn't your wit slow or feeble? And isn't every part of your body attacked by the aging process?

So what is our response to all of these questions? At some point in our lives, we must answer yes to all of them if we live long enough. How do we react to the bleakness of the human condition and the inevitability of our mortality? Will we ever be able to dispel our fears and summon up the strength and courage to face the inevitable ravages of time?

Many existentialists and nihilists have a pessimistic outlook on life. They emphasize the meaninglessness of human existence. In their way of reckoning, there is no God, no divine providence. If there were a God, why does evil defeat good with such regularity? they ask. Therefore, they insist that the sum total of man's strivings on planet earth is indiscriminate pain and suffering punctuated by a few snippets of pleasure here and there. And so, their contention is that our sojourn on this earth is characterized by nothingness and absurdity, with change, decay, and death being the only constant. However, those of us who believe in God share an entirely different view of the human condition. We believe that evil will endure for a while but will be eradicated eventually by God—the Ultimate Force of Good. Therefore, we have a hope. Being mortals, we know we must endure pain and suffering in life and eventually succumb to our mortality. However, death is not the final chapter. There is eternal life beyond the "sleep" to which Shakespeare refers.

We Are Such Stuff

We are such stuff
As dreams are made on, and our little life
Is rounded with a sleep.
(*The Tempest* 4. 1. 156-58)

PARAPHRASE

We humans go through life like characters we encounter in our dreams (or perhaps nightmares in some instances). And the short life we spend on this earth is circular in scope, in that we begin in oblivion, asleep in our mothers' wombs and eventually return to sleep once more in the womb of Mother Earth when we die, when our lives are ended or "rounded" in oblivion.

Tomorrow, and Tomorrow, and Tomorrow

Tomorrow, and tomorrow, and tomorrow
Creeps in this petty pace from day to day,
To the last syllable of recorded time,
And all our yesterdays have lighted fools
The way to dusty death. Out, out, brief candle!
Life's but a walking shadow, a poor player
That struts and frets his hour upon the stage
And then is heard no more. It is a tale
Told by an idiot, full of sound and fury,
Signifying nothing.
(*Macbeth 5. 5. 19-28)*

PARAPHRASE

Here, Shakespeare laments the human condition. He comments on the vanity of human existence. He says:

The days of our lives follow one another in slow succession and will continue to do so until the final chapter of earth's history. And each day, from the inception of this earth, has dispatched defenseless humans and sent them to their deaths. Life is a fragile candle that swiftly blows out. It is as unsubstantial as a moving shade or shadow. It is ineffectual and short-lived as an unskilled actor who swaggers and fusses for an allotted hour on a stage and is then burnt out. Life could be compared to a fictitious narrative—a fable— narrated by someone with diminished mental faculties, one who fusses, babbles, and makes meaningless noises which amount to nothing.

As Flies to Wanton Boys

As flies to wanton boys are we to the gods,

They kill us for their sport.
(*King Lear* 4. 1. 38-39)

PARAPHRASE

In the eyes of the gods,* we humans are as unimportant as flies are to wicked boys. The gods kill us to amuse themselves just as mischievous boys kill flies for their amusement.

***NOTE:** Shakespeare is reminding us that the ancients—the pagans—believed that the affairs of mankind were governed by the dictates, even the whims, of many gods. The ancient Greeks and Romans, for example, believed themselves to be at the mercy of their myriad anthropomorphic gods whose will they frequently elicited through the Oracle at Delphi (believed to be the priest of Apollo).

Of All My Lands

...of all my lands
Is nothing left me but my body's length.
Why, what is pomp, rule, reign, but earth and dust?
And, live we how we can, yet die we must.
(3 *Henry VI* 5. 2. 25-28)

PARAPHRASE

In spite of my many possessions, I actually own nothing except the space my body occupies or will occupy (the grave). What good is spectacle, grandeur, dominion, and majesty but empty, worthless dirt and ashes? We mortals can achieve the loftiest form of existence (actually, we can live any way we wish), but death is a must for all.

For God's Sake, Let Us Sit

For God's sake, let us sit upon the ground
And tell sad stories of the death of kings---
How some have been deposed, some slain in war,
Some haunted by the ghosts they have deposed,
Some poisoned by their wives, some sleeping killed,
All murdered. For within the hollow crown
That rounds the mortal temples of a king
Keeps Death his Court, and there the antic sits,
Scoffing his state and grinning at his pomp,
Allowing him a breath, a little scene,
To monarchize , be feared, and kill with looks,
Infusing him with self and vain conceit,
As if this flesh which walls about our life
Were brass impregnable, and humored thus
Comes at the last and with a little pin
Bores through his castle wall, and farewell King!
(*Richard II* 3. 2. 155-70)

PARAPHRASE

Once more, Shakespeare reminds us of our human condition—our fragile existence in spite of our pomp and circumstance:

For God's sake, let us sit on the ground and tell unhappy tales of the demise of monarchs—some of whom have been overthrown, some killed in battle, some tormented by the spirits of rulers they have unseated, some poisoned by their wives, some slain while asleep. They were all assassinated because in the circular cavity of the crown that covers the head of any king on this earth, Death sets up his domain, and there this grotesque character sits laughing, mocking, taunting, and ridiculing the king's stately demeanor and his show of splendor and dignity. Death gives the king a little time and a little space to show off his power and majesty while those around him fear him and are overcome by his mere looks. Death toys with him further by filling him with selfish pride, egotism, and arrogance, causing him to think that his body is an unassailable fortress. And while the king is thus deceived, Death comes eventually and, with little or no effort, penetrates the king's defenses; it is then goodbye King!

All the World's a Stage

All the world's a stage,
And all the men and women merely players.
They have their exits and their entrances,
And one man in his time plays many parts,
His acts being seven ages. At first the infant,
Mewling and puking in the nurse's arms.
Then the whining schoolboy, with his satchel
And shining morning face, creeping like snail
Unwillingly to school. And then the lover,
Sighing like furnace, with a woeful ballad
Made to his mistress' eyebrow. Then a soldier,
Full of strange oaths and bearded like the pard,
Jealous in honor, sudden and quick in quarrel,
Seeking the bubble reputation
Even in the cannon's mouth. And then the justice,
In fair round belly with good capon lined,
With eyes severe and beard of formal cut,
Full of wise saws and modern instances,
And so he plays his part. The sixth age shifts
Into the lean and slippered Pantaloon
With spectacles on nose and pouch on side,

His youthful hose, well saved, a world too wide
For his shrunk shank, and his big manly voice,
Turning again toward childish treble, pipes
And whistles in his sound. Last scene of all,
That ends this strange eventful history,
Is second childishness and mere oblivion,
Sans teeth, sans eyes, sans taste, sans everything.
(*As You Like It* 2. 7. 139-66)

PARAPHRASE

In these famous lines, Shakespeare captures the cyclical nature of the human condition. He presents seven stages of life: the infant, the adolescent, the lover, the soldier, the judge, the senior citizen, and finally the second infant whose decrepit life is a precursor of death. Shakespeare declares that our world is a metaphorical stage, and as we interact from day to day, we are simply characters moving about and going on and off the stage of life, and one man (or one human being) plays many roles in his (or her) existence. His life is divided into seven acts or scenes. First he is a baby whimpering and spitting up in his caretaker's arms. Then he is a bright-faced school boy with his book bag, going slowly and reluctantly to school, complaining as he goes. Next, he is a passionate, hot-blooded lover, spouting flattering words and composing bad love songs to praise his lover's eyebrows. As a soldier, he makes many remarkable promises and is as confrontational as the leopard. Sensitive to matters concerning his honor, he is ever ready to defend himself in any dispute. He would risk his life, even placing himself in front of a cannon to achieve empty, shortlived esteem. Next, this "everyman" is a judge with a fairly large round belly that is filled with the tasty flesh of a castrated rooster. His eyes are stern and his beard is trimmed neatly and officially. He has many wise sayings and commonplace anecdotes, as he functions in his role. In the sixth stage of his life, he is a thin old man in slippers and baggy trousers, with glasses on his nose and his wallet at his side. His breeches from his younger days are still in good shape, but they are far too big for his shriveled legs, and his voice which was once deep and resonant is becoming high-pitched once more like a child's. It is high-toned and shrill when he speaks. The final stage in this full and remarkable life is second infancy and absolute senility, without teeth, without eyesight, without taste buds (appetite), without everything.

Meeting in Heaven

The hour of death is expiate.
Come, Grey, come, Vaughan, let us all embrace,
And take our leave until we meet in Heaven.
(*Richard* III 3. 3. 23-25)

PARAPHRASE

The hour of death has arrived. Come Grey and Vaughn, let us hug one another and say goodbye until we meet in heaven. The human condition does not end in death but in eternal life in heaven. This is the message here.

COMMENTARY: Childhood Fears of Death in Montserrat and Reassurance of Life In Heaven

If the question were asked, What do humans fear most, the answer arguably would be death. Most humans would relinquish all possessions in order to cling to life. The ancient Egyptians aspired to immortality through mummification, seeking to keep death at bay for as long as possible. They believed that the dead would begin a new life in another world. This new life would be similar to the life on earth, and so the mummified body would provide a house for the spirit as it crossed over from this earthly life to the after life. So what is the modern perception of death? Why does this phenomenon terrify us so? It is an ever-present, dismal reminder of our human condition. Little wonder that, to me, New Year's Eve is the saddest day of each year. Even as the world watches and waits in raucous jubilation for balls to descend and fireworks to light up the sky, I stare into the future without seeing. I am usually unable to shake the haunting realization that a year looms large on the horizon teeming with unknown, unexpected, uncontrollable, possibly inescapable events that we are "heir to," as Shakespeare puts it. For example, just the other day, two young Hollywood idols/icons—Michael Jackson and Farrah Fawcett—died on the very same day. Fame, adulation, and money could not help them escape the human condition. And what about the frequently-occurring tsunamis and tornadoes—literal as well as figurative—that leave so much death and destruction behind as they spiral forward relentlessly? The human condition is the answer.

    As a child growing up in Montserrat, West Indies, I struggled to grasp the concept of death. I remember my very first wake (the custom of sitting all night with the dead before the funeral the following day). On that night, my first wake, we were all singing hymns and crying. My mother, my sisters, and the villagers had gathered to watch with the dead. I remember the "Woo Woo" dance—a dance involving a person entranced, swirling around the room, allegedly making contact with the spirit world while someone played an ancient wood instrument that made a loud, monotonous , mournful sound. At these wakes, I was often equally terrified of the living as I was of the dead. Because my family was enlightened and religious, we never had "Woo Woo" dancing at our funerals, only singing and crying.

When my sister and mother passed away, I recall our wakes in Montserrat, as their bodies lay in state in the middle of our living room in all the starkness and the cold reality of death. The neighbors came on those nights to pay their respect. I remember an irrational, inexplicable feeling of embarrassment intruding on my consciousness when the villagers stared down at my mother and sister. I didn't want anyone to look at them. Did I have this feeling because my childhood vulnerability and fear of death had encroached on my adult perception, leaving me self-conscious? Or was it because, from an early age, I had recognized the meaninglessness—the vanity—of human existence? We "strut" and "fret" for most of our lives, even exhibiting pomp, circumstance, and hubris, only to fall so quickly after birth into a state of oblivion, money and fame notwithstanding. So how can we defeat this oblivion? How can we transcend our mortality? Is there eternal life after death? Is there a heaven conferring immortality on us mortals after we exit this life?

So many mortals have searched and continue to search systematically to find an answer to these questions. Millions of Americans flocked to watch a Barbara Walters Special that aired on ABC on December 20, 2005, titled "Heaven, Where Is It? How Do We Get There?" Walters indicated that she had labored for approximately a year to produce this special designed to clarify the mystery of heaven, and she confessed that she cared about this project more "than anything else" she had done. She interviewed many famous personalities, asking them the seminal question: "Is heaven an actual place or a myth?" Her research revealed that nine out of every ten Americans believe heaven exists, and most expect to go there after death, in spite of the conditions outlined in the Bible.

Unfortunately, it was not possible for Barbara Walters to interview Shakespeare, but if she could have, she might have discovered that the characters in his plays actually voice his beliefs. And even if he has put words that he did not endorse in their mouths, those words reveal ideas that were popular in his age. The following statements are among those he has made that demonstrate belief in the existence of heaven. In *Richard III* one character says to his companions: " The hour of death is expiate" (has arrived). His companion responds: ". . . let us all embrace, / And take our leave until we meet in heaven" (3. 3. 23-25). Shakespeare's references to heaven are numerous. Two other examples will suffice: In *Measure for Measure,* one character exhorts another. Don't despair, he encourages, "give your cause to Heaven" (4. 3. 129). Similarly, the ghost of Hamlet's father does not ask his son to seek vengeance against his unfaithful wife (Hamlet's mother). "Leave her to heaven," he advises (*Hamlet* 1. 5. 86).

Like Shakespeare, other writers have accepted the possibility of life after this one on planet earth. John Milton writes assuredly: "Death be not proud! A short sleep, and I will wake again, eternally. A short voyage, and I will meet my Maker face to face." Similarly, Leo Tolstoy affirms: "Love is God, and to die means that I, a particle of love, shall return to the general eternal source." William Wordsworth expresses that same thought in his famous "Ode: Intimations of Immortality." He declares: ". . . trailing clouds of glory do we come / From God, who is our home:/ Heaven lies about us in our infancy!" And heaven is our final destination. Therefore, those of us who are believers in God should not view death with the dismal trepidation, foreboding, and hopelessness as non-believers. Instead, we should see death for what it is: a gateway to return to God who is our home.

It is terrifying to think of dying without the hope of living again in a place called heaven. After all the pain and the travail, actually even if life were all pleasure, if the human lot were to die and enter a state of oblivion, forever, what a sad thought that would be. It is wonderful to know that there is a place where mortals can have a second chance at life, no longer oppressed by the human condition but enjoying, instead, a blissful existence forever.

Our greatest challenge is to cultivate a new image of death. Will we poor mortals ever be able to embrace the idea that there is no reason for us to fear death? Death's dominion should dissipate, and we should revel in the hope of future immortality in heaven whenever we hear the following reassuring words of Christ reminding us that heaven is within the reach of all who strive to get there. He encourages us to believe in Him and be faithful:

> Let not your heart be troubled: ye believe in God, believe also in me. In my Father's house are many mansions: if it were not so, I would have told you. I go to prepare a place for you. And if I go and prepare a place for you, I will come again, and receive you unto myself; that where I am, there ye may be also. (St. John 14: 1-3)

4. ADVERSITY

INTRODUCTION

It has been said, albeit flippantly, that even the most devout atheist calls on God when he or she is in trouble. Another accepted conceit is that no one can be cheerful when everything goes wrong. Not even the iconic Job—that paragon of patience—could endure adversity without lamenting. He lost all of his children, all of his servants, and all of his abundant wealth. He even lost his good health, yet he never lost faith in God. "Though He slay me, yet will I trust in Him," he resolves (Job 13: 15). But even this master of faith, this stalwart, had moments of dark depression that caused him to question the ways of God. How many of us can go "placidly" and cheerily through life in the face of disaster? Not many. Perhaps I should say, not any. And yet, adversity is a constant on planet earth. Adversity undergirds practically all of Shakespeare's plays, even the comedies, for the simple reason that it is the human lot to encounter adverse circumstances. One or two examples will suffice. A king is murdered by his own brother who also seduces and marries the king's wife (*Hamlet*). A duke is exiled by his brother who usurps his throne (*As You Like It*). Unrequited love causes much pain in *A Midsummer Night's Dream*. A father is maltreated by two of his daughters and is driven to homelessness and lunacy (*King Lear*).

Fiction mirrors reality, and so like reality, it turns on adversity. Just think, even the fairy tales that were read to us as children are rife with adversity, and even though most of them end happily ever after, what punishment those poor characters go through. A beautiful girl must endure grueling labor and the scorn and ridicule of her ugly, older step-sisters and stepmother before her fairy godmother and Prince Charming finally arrive to deliver her. Another beautiful fairytale heroine is sentenced to death. She is chased from her home and forced to live in exile simply because she is more beautiful than her stepmother, the queen. Another character deems it right to exert his superior power and seeks to "huff and puff" and blow down the houses of his defenseless neighbors, just because he is big and bad. We watched the lovely Lady Diana Spencer meet and marry her prince who transformed her into the archetypal fairy princess. Well, we know how that fairytale ended.

In our everyday world, all it takes is the flick of a television switch or a glance at the newspaper headlines to discern that adversity is ubiquitous and non-discriminating in its reach. Rich, poor, old, young, religious, and non-religious are all its victims. A number of wealthy people in California lose their mansions in devastating fires. Time and time again, monster tornadoes destroy lives and demolish the homes, cars, and other possessions of families in various states in America. A few days ago, the mother of five young children was shot to death as she shopped in a department store. Not long ago, two sisters were killed while worshipping at a church in Florida.

The incidents that document ever-present adversity are too many to recount here. What about that apocalyptic, all-consuming, mammoth earthquake and tsunami that decimated communities in Japan on March 11, 2011? That day, we watched our television screens in speechless terror and disbelief. We saw vegetation, cars, large houses, ships, even passenger trains being propelled effortlessly by a mighty tidal wave that liquified the land mass and reduced it to a gargantuan ocean of floating objects that looked like tiny, bobbing toys in a child's bathtub. That day, we were reminded that we are living in the final days of earth's history. That day, how puny, how evanescent, how inconsequential things of this world appeared. All that mattered was the need to prepare to occupy that other land where tsunamis, earthquakes, hurricanes, and all other disasters—natural or man-made—are non-existent. As I watched the colossal loss of life that day, my recurrent thought was the vanity of human existence—the fact that majestic, sturdily built cities could be reduced to rubble in mere minutes by the unbridled forces in nature.

These are but a few incidents referenced to emphasize the fact that adversity is often indiscriminate, overwhelming, and inescapable. When it rears its ugly head, all we can do is lament and ask a question that has no answer: Why? Why do the good suffer right along with the bad? As we struggle to find a satisfactory answer to this question, we should determine to surround ourselves with one or two proverbial, accessible "lifeboats" to which we can cling and save ourselves when our life's ship is sinking after being struck by adversity. In other words, we should prepare ourselves from this day forth to fight. The best way to fight or rise above adversity is to cultivate or generate the strength to make something positive out of a negative situation; to draw some measure of good from a bad circumstance; to look for and actually find something constructive or worthwhile to do or hold on to when life's physical, mental, and emotional tsunamis strike. Oh, I am the first to admit that all of this is difficult to achieve, but we should put forth every effort not to sink beneath the weight of despair. We should get up, get busy, set ourselves some worthwhile goal—no matter how small—and pursue it.

Let me demonstrate what I mean. What could be more demoralizing, distressing, and heart-wrenching than losing one's freedom (particularly when innocent)? Even the lower animals do not thrive in captivity. And yet, John Bunyan wrote his masterpiece, *The Pilgrim's Progress* (1678) while he was incarcerated. He was torn from his family and friends; he was alone and disheartened, but he never lost faith or the will to live or the desire to preach. He must have said to himself, "Aha, let me use all of this time I have on my hands while in prison to write a book." Millions of copies of this book have been sold, and it is considered the most famous allegory depicting mankind's journey on the treacherous, rocky pathway of life. The protagonist (who represents Everyman) travels until he reaches his eventual destination: heaven. And so, Bunyan used his misfortune to create a literary beacon that has guided Christians and non-Christians alike.

A Wretched Soul Bruised

A wretched soul, bruised with adversity,
We bid be quiet when we hear it cry;
But were we burdened with like weight of pain,
As much, or more, we should ourselves complain.
So thou, that hast no unkind mate to grieve thee,
With urging helpless patience wouldst relieve me.

But if thou live to see like right bereft,
This fool-begged patience in thee will be left.
(*The Comedy of Errors* 2. 1. 34-41)

PARAPHRASE

When we hear the lament of a miserable soul injured by misfortune, we tell it to be silent. However, if we were suffering in like manner, we would whine or protest as much or even more. Therefore, those of you who don't have mean or insensitive spouses to upset you, would seek to pacify me by advocating patience which is futile. But if you were to live long enough to see yourself treated as I am (i.e. to see your rights also taken away), you would soon abandon this silly plea for patience.

Sweet Are the Uses of Adversity

Sweet are the uses of adversity,
Which, like the toad, ugly and venomous,
Wears yet a precious jewel in his head.
And this our life exempt from public haunt
Finds tongues in trees, books in the running brooks,
Sermons in stones, and good in everything.
I would not change it.
(*As You Like It* 2. 1. 12-18)

In these lines, a deposed and exiled duke is admitting that adversity could sometimes yield a measure of peace and contentment. In some instances, adversity does build maturity and strength of character.

PARAPHRASE

There are some benefits to be derived from adversity in the same way that a hideous, poisonous frog carries a gem in its head. (This was a common belief in Shakespeare's day.) And in the pastoral life that we now live—far removed from crowds, free from noise and confusion—we can learn valuable lessons from nature: We can glean knowledge and comfort from the trees, the streams, and the stones. In fact, we can derive satisfaction from everything that surrounds us. I don't wish to change anything.

Let Me Embrace Thee, Sour Adversity

Let me embrace thee, sour Adversity,
For wise men say it is the wisest course.
(3 *Henry VI* 3. 1. 24-25)

PARAPHRASE

Adversity, you are bitter and repulsive, and yet I will welcome or accept you because wise people say that's the best thing to do.

COMMENTARY: Half an Island Paradise Is Better Than None

Since adversity is an inescapable part of our human experience, the words "welcome or accept" in the preceding paraphrase simply means cultivating the strength to turn negatives into positives. This is something we humans must learn to do if we are to survive on planet earth. On April 29, 2011, a classic fairytale actually morphed into reality before our very eyes as the English Prince Charming chose his princess from among the "commoners." However, as millions watched in America, they saw a haunting split screen on television. The devastation, mass destruction, and misery caused by several monster tornadoes that had leveled many communities in America appeared side by side with the epitome of earthly privilege and luxury at that wedding. It was as if Destiny was saying mockingly: "Hey world, here's a contrast! On planet earth, in mere moments, you can go from this to this. Be warned!" And having been warned, we must make a conscientious effort to survive after adversity. We must cultivate and strengthen our will to live—to go on after sickness, divorce, death, and misfortune of any kind. We have an intuitive urge to get up after falling developed from our toddler stage. I call this urge our natural buoyancy which should kick in after every adversity. Therefore, let me share my motto with you, my readers: <u>Let your natural or intuitive buoyancy conquer or at least reduce your adversity.</u>

One of the most fascinating examples of buoyancy after adversity is seen in the experience of the courageous Montserratians. Here is their story. The small British island of Montserrat in the Caribbean is a dramatic study in resilience after two major disasters. In September 1989, Montserrat was transformed into a wasteland by a monstrous hurricane named Hugo. The cyclonic winds toppled massive trees that had decorated the landscape for decades and leveled houses big and small. Like two marauding demons, the wind and the rain seemed to conspire to reduce all thirty-two square miles of this tiny island to instant rubble. Churches, schools, government buildings, and homes all succumbed to the ravages of these two fiends. A number of lives were lost, and the Montserratian way of life seemed to have reverted to that of the Middle Ages, as the victims of Hugo struggled to provide food and shelter and regain their collective equilibrium. One of the most astounding consequences of the storm, discerned in its aftermath, was the starkness of the landscape. This fertile island—known for its cornucopia of fruits and vegetables, its lush green fields, and majestic mountain range—was reduced to a barren, treeless expanse. Fortunately, the islanders stumbled around in bewilderment for only a brief time. With characteristic resurgence, they resolved to rebuild with help from Mother England as well as neighboring islands such as Dominica, Bermuda, Barbados, Bahamas, Grenada, Trinidad, and others. In less than no time, a mammoth reconstruction effort was in progress. The islanders united and, with a monolithic arm, reversed much of the ravages of Hugo.

But Mother Nature was not done with Montserrat. Soufrière, a volcano which was dormant for decades even before I was born, suddenly erupted in 1995. From the mountain range came a torrential downpour of molten rocks and ash. But the pyroclastic flow was the killer. It was a relentless flow of liquid fire consuming everything in its path: humans, animals, trees and other vegetation as well as houses and even large commercial buildings. Within a relatively brief period, the entire southern half of the island of Montserrat was demolished. Somehow, this liquid fiery demon seemed to target the élan vital—the life source—of the island, swallowing up the urban area and its suburbs: the town of Plymouth with the only hospital, the airport, the seaport, the banks, the civic structures, the major churches, schools, and stores. Imagine the loss of homes. Imagine the pain when Montserratians had to accept the reality that their beloved island was reduced to almost one-third of its size because, for safety reasons, it became illegal even to visit the barren wasteland that was the southern and eastern parts of Montserrat. Once more, England intervened and offered asylum to her subjects.

The majority of Montserratians abandoned the island and relocated in England, Canada, and America as well as other Caribbean islands. For many years, the authorities urged evacuation. However, to this very day, a number of courageous, patriotic Montserratians cling tenaciously to their cherished homeland.. This destructive volcano is a heart-wrenching realization even for those of us who have not lived in Montserrat since childhood. The volcano is still a lurking presence. Even now, almost daily, volcanic ash falls on houses, cars, trees, and all in its path.

However, the intriguing aspect of this dilemma is that the ever-resilient Montserratians have stared down adversity and have made a concerted, collective effort to survive. They have moved the commercial hub and the seat of government to the northern part of the island. They have built new homes and new industrial buildings in northern Montserrat which is now a tourist attraction. Many visitors are quite possibly curious to see the brave souls who have defied the volcano and have refused to surrender their beloved island to this natural intruder. Actually, a number of Montserratians who evacuated years ago have returned to take up residence once more in Montserrat. Other strong, admirable, resilient Montserratians who lost their beautiful homes and other possessions to the volcano did not relinquish the will to live and fight. Instead, by dint of hard work, they have acquired new homes in America and elsewhere.

In our human existence, though adversity is normalcy and is, therefore, widespread, we regard those who have battled immense losses and excruciating pain with enduring respect. These are the people who have acquired the fortitude, the buoyancy, to rise above adversity, treating "Triumph and Disaster…just the same," as Rudyard Kipling so eloquently puts it in his brilliant poem, "If". At times of adversity, we can be heartened as we listen to God's promise in the following words; they should help us summon up the buoyancy we need to overcome:

> When thou passest through the waters, I will
> be with thee; and through the rivers, they shall
> not overflow thee: when thou walkest through
> the fire, thou shalt not be burned; neither shall

the flame kindle upon thee…. Fear
not: for I am with thee:
(*Isaiah* 43: 2; 5)

5. STUDY---EDUCATION

INTRODUCTION

As I turn my attention to education, I would be remiss if I did not pause to say thank you to America for the significant role she has played in my education. I never hesitate to affirm vociferously, "God bless America!" I cannot speak for the millions around the globe whose lives have been touched by the beneficence, altruism, and magnanimity of this great country in its myriad charitable outreaches and projects. However, I can speak as one who has benefited first hand, dating back to my early school days in the Caribbean. As a young child in Montserrat, I watched American volunteers distributing buns and cups of hot chocolate early each morning at my elementary school, courtesy of the American Red Cross. For me, the term "all you can eat" had its inception here. The volunteers made sure we started each school day with full stomachs so that we could better absorb what we were taught. Though some students did not need this meal, to the majority, it was a necessity. I also saw many large boxes with powdered milk being unloaded from trucks. Each box had the inscription:"United States of America." In addition to the meals, the American Red Cross provided tutoring in first aid and general health.

In the island of Antigua, the American presence was palpable. It was seen in the two ample bases (army and navy) that America established there during World War II when she came on the scene to liberate Europe and the rest of the world from the Nazis. The Americans built macadamized roads and refurbished the airport. They built schools, factories, large plantations, beautiful hotels, and retail stores, all of which provided full time jobs for many Antiguans. As a matter of fact, largely because of America, in those early years, Antigua became a mecca in the Leeward Islands, as many residents of the other islands flocked there seeking employment and better lives for their families. My father was one such immigrant. A number of American-owned sugar cane plantations decorated the Antiguan countryside, providing a livelihood for the laborers in the fields as well as the sugar cane factory.

I recall my school days when I lived on the Judges Sugar Cane Plantation where my father was employed as an overseer. The modest house provided for my father was surrounded by miles and miles of sugar cane plants, rising profusely, stretching as far as the eye could see. As a child at Judges, I enjoyed some memorable moments. Chief among them, I can remember the overloaded tractors piled high with the sugar cane plants freshly cut by the energetic workers. Even as I write, I can see once more each fully-loaded tractor wending its way slowly, laboriously to the factory. I watch the marauding bands of school children descend upon the tractor, shrieking in glee, as they hold on to any accessible sugar cane plant. They methodically pull as many as they can from the tractor and eagerly sink their teeth in the pulp to extract the delicious nectar from the sugar cane plant while the tractor-driver turns an obliging blind eye to their maneuvers. His attitude is live and let live, courtesy of America.

My adolescent recollections take me to another scene in my school days when America had a significant impact. When I was a student at the Antigua Girls' High School in the city of St. John's, each Christmas season, the American Red Cross Society sponsored a "Driving with Santa" outreach. This effort entailed a large donation of toys by the Americans. One day in each December was set aside for an American Santa Claus to drive around the island of Antigua, delivering toys to disadvantaged children. I was one of the privileged High School girls who usually drove in Santa's entourage. We rode high atop a large, open truck, singing gleefully such songs as "Santa Claus Is Coming to Town," as we approached each village. I am not sure who derived more pleasure—those grateful, excited children or we who brought the Christmas cheer to them, courtesy of America.

Reference could be made to several other Caribbean nations where America has made an impact on education. However, one other example will suffice. Several years ago, when I was a Ph. D. candidate at the University of Miami, I participated in the extra-mural, outreach program run by the University of Miami whereby teachers in the Bahamas could earn a bachelor's degree from the University of Miami without leaving the Bahamas to take classes. The English Department at the University of Miami sent me on a mission to teach literature to Bahamian teachers who were enrolled in this summer program. That assignment was no picnic. I did not visit any of the beautiful beaches. Instead, I spent the entire allotted number of weeks working hard to fortify the skills of those teachers and help them launch successful careers, once more courtesy of America.

The point I am seeking to emphasize is the fact that in Antigua, Montserrat, and various other Caribbean islands, America facilitated our education, and she did so without pillage, without occupation, without annexation, without deriving any political advantage. Though some may opine to the contrary, world records show that this spontaneous, free giving is the American way. Whenever I say thank you to America, I must simultaneously say thank you to one of my sisters—Mariel—the only one fortunate enough to have been born in one of the American Virgin Islands. As a resident of New York, she worked hard to enable our survival during my formative years. The Red Cross packages that went to the schools in Montserrat were no more frequent than the packages she mailed, by dint of hard labor, to our home in Montserrat. She not only helped significantly with our day to day subsistence; she also supplied us with equipment for school.

I will be forever proud of, and grateful for, the solid, sterling British educational foundation I received in the islands of Antigua and Montserrat. As a school girl, I sang with gusto and national pride "God Save Our Gracious Queen," "Rule Britannia," "Heart of Oak Are Our Ships," and many other songs that bestowed well-deserved honor on good old Mother England. However, I often sang with equal energy and gratitude songs like "O Beautiful for Spacious Skies…. America, America God shed His grace on thee and crown thy good with brotherhood from sea to shining sea." I am one naturalized American citizen who says, thank you America even as I say, thank you England.

One legacy which I hold dear is my British study ethic. It was during my formative years in the Caribbean that I acquired the tenacity to overcome the challenges and adversities I encountered in my later academic pursuits. I was taught early to strive for excellence, and when I became an educator, I determined to pass on to my students the same resolve to excel and achieve. Shakespeare emphasizes the need for excellence in education. He stresses the phenomenal benefit of a solid education by labeling it a "godlike recompense." Therefore, it is with a measure of sadness that I have had to accept the fact that for decades, students with sub-elementary skills are being graduated from many of our high schools across the nation. In February 2008, a startling piece of news hit the air waves. In a high school in Florida, the entire faculty and administration were fired because the vast majority of students at that school continually failed all state examinations. At another school somewhere in Georgia, the teachers and administrators regularly gave the students the answers to standardized tests so that the school could look good. Little wonder that a significant number of national newspapers and television broadcasts have documented the fact that many high school graduates, across America, are incapable of communicating in coherent grammatical sentences and are unable to read with facility and comprehension. Many of these students populate college classrooms across the nation, victims of severely inflated grades and unmerited promotion. As a result, writing labs, remedial classes, and other developmental programs have become a constant on college campuses.

Another consequence of grade inflation on college campuses is the emergence of a crusade against those professors whom I term the "Toughies." At the college where I taught for many years, from day one, I was considered "Toughie Number One" by students and colleagues alike.. Professors like me have been made to feel that we are unnecessarily stringent; that the A's we award are far too few; that our C's have the value of A's from other colleagues; that we fail to pass students for effort regardless of their substandard performance. Of course, I have managed to resist this line of reasoning, but I must admit that once or twice I was persuaded to relax my grading slightly.

One day, a few years ago, as I sat in my office on my college campus, I was impelled to write about the damaging effects of grade inflation, the fact that it deprives our students of the skills they need in the world of work. I found myself thinking of Cain's answer when he was asked about his brother Abel. "Am I my brother's keeper?" was his perfunctory reply (*Genesis 4:9*). That day, I was confronted with the realization that, to a large degree, we professors are the academic "keepers" of our youth. I, therefore, wrote an article entitled, "The Cain Principle: Am I My Students' Keeper?" I decided to use this article as my Commentary in this chapter. Shortly after writing this article, I found a book whose author is also concerned about the inadequate academic preparation of America's youth. She laments the fact that the majority of her colleagues deem it appropriate to hand out A's to failing students in order to boost their self-esteem and keep them from complaining. The title of this timely book is The Feel-Good Curriculum: The Dumbing Down of America's Kids in the Name of Self-Esteem by Maureen Stout. Obviously, Shakespeare, were he alive today, would share our concern.

What Is the End of Study?

Berowne: What is the end of study? Let me know.

King: Why, that to know which else we should not know.

Berowne: Things hid and barred, you mean, from common sense?

King: Aye, that is study's godlike recompense.
(*Love's Labor's Lost* 1.1. 55-58)

PARAPHRASE

Berowne: Let me know what benefits may be derived from studying.

King: When we study, we acquire knowledge that we would otherwise not gain.

Berowne: Do you mean information outside the realm of mere intuition?

King: Yes, that is the almost superhuman attribute (reward) we derive from studying.

Study Is Like the Heaven's Glorious Sun

Study is like the heaven's glorious sun,
That will not be deep-searched with saucy looks.
Small have continual plodders ever won,
Save base authority from others' books.
(*Love's Labor's Lost* 1. 1. 84-87)

PARAPHRASE

In a nutshell, Shakespeare is saying that knowledge is so vast that even a small amount requires much study:

Seeking to acquire all knowledge through studying is as unrealistic as seeking to penetrate or comprehend the glory and mystery of the sun. No amount of research or deep presumptuous probing can yield such vast, unattainable knowledge. Even those that research and investigate regularly have gleaned very little beyond basic bits of information in books written by other people.

My Years Are Young

....[M]y years are young!
And fitter is my study and my books
Than wanton dalliance with a paramour.
(I *Henry* VI 5. 1. 21-23)

PARAPHRASE

I am young! And during my youth, it is more appropriate to focus on my studies and my books instead of wasting time in frivolous amorous pursuits.

Some Food We Had

Some food we had, and some fresh water, that
A noble Neapolitan, Gonzalo,
Out of his charity. . .did give us, with
Rich garments, linens, stuffs, and necessaries,
Which since have steaded much. So, of his gentle-
    ness,
Knowing I loved my books, he furnished me
From mine own library with volumes that
I prize above my dukedom.
(*The Tempest* 1. 2. 160-68)

PARAPHRASE

Out of the goodness of his heart, Gonzalo, a noble Neapolitan, gave us some food and fresh water. He also gave us expensive clothes, linen, and other accessories and necessities which have helped tremendously. Also, because of his kindness, knowing how much I valued my books, he provided me with many books from my own library—books that I treasure more than my dukedom.

COMMENTARY:

In the preceding passage, a duke places greater value on his books than on his entire dukedom. How unusual! Would modern students choose their books over their cars or any other valuable possessions? Fortunately, they don't have to make that choice. In the typical classroom, they are simply expected to demonstrate that they have at least minimum passing skill in the subjects taught. I decided to share with my readers the following article which I wrote on February 17, 2003.

The Cain Principle: Am I My Students' Keeper?

I am sitting in my office. It is the last hour of the allotted time to submit my end-of-term grades. Beads of perspiration blanket my face. My computer seems to look on sympathetically as I read and reread segments of students' essays. Finally, I award a "C" to a student who really deserves a "D"; a "D" to a student who truly deserves an "F"; "B" to a student who deserves a "C", and surprisingly I give a student who deserves a "B" an "A". I am uncomfortable when I leave my office. My discomfiture persists throughout my vacation. The troubling thought is that my grading is less stringent than it was before. Throughout my years as a college professor, my students and my colleagues have labeled me "too tough." One day, a student approached me: "Dr. Charles, do you know you have a reputation on campus?" she asked. I blanched instinctively but without cause. She was referring to my tough grading policy. Recently, however, I decided to relax my grading scale marginally, but I am uncomfortable in doing so. Year after year I have been appalled as I watch the dire consequences of inflated grading and social promotion in the academic world. This grade-inflation epidemic flourishes as a pervasive disease that may have infected even the toughest among us, educators.

I remember when I strode into my first college classroom as a newly-hired adjunct instructor of English at Lehman College in New York. Quixotic in demeanor and expectation, I was ready to do battle with Chaucer, Milton, Shakespeare, Hemingway, Plato, Aristotle, Virgil, and other literary giants. However, I soon discovered that the pygmy-sized mechanics of the English language were the adversaries of my students and were, therefore, the windmills I had to topple.

Born in a British Caribbean Island, I was schooled in an educational system that emphasized excellence. There was no grading on the curve; no social promotion; no grade inflation. We had to master the material if we hoped to move from one level to another. As an instructor and professor in America, I carried these identical principles and expectations into my classrooms to this day. But recently, I have discovered that I have succumbed to the temptation to let one or two students slide by with slightly higher grades than the ones deserved. Naturally, these students are pleased when they receive satisfactory grades. They feel good about themselves. So why am I uncomfortable?

In my reflection and self probing, I focus on the mission of my college and my individual duty to my students. I ask myself, Am I commissioned to make students feel good, building pseudo self-esteem, or am I in the classroom to give them honest feedback and grades they truly earn, while I strengthen their communication skills? I know the answer. I recognize that my mission is to encourage my students, to engender responsibility and maturity in them that they will accept any low grades that they earn and strive to develop the proficiency that warrants higher grades, while they enjoy the self confidence that accompanies true competence.

So why was I less exacting on one or two occasions and more compromising in assessing my students' performance? In my soul searching, I recall Cain's indifferent response when he was asked about his brother: "Am I my brother's keeper?" he asked. If we, professors, see ourselves as the primary contributors to our students' academic well being, then we must determine unequivocally whether we are our students' keepers. Additionally, we must analyze what "keepership" entails, recognizing that grade inflation is counterproductive. **We need to realize that we are preparing our students to compete with students from various parts of the world.** Inflated grades build a false feeling of achievement, creating short term well being but long term disillusionment when students later discover their inadequacy and realize that their performance is not commensurate with their grades.

Yet social promotion and unwarranted boosting of grades is a problem that persists in the school system as well as in many community colleges and even universities. In certain colleges, for example, some professors buckle under the pressure plied by administrators who insist that they be shown that professors have achieved retention in their classes. Retention! Retention is the byword! Retention at all cost! And why not, when the state provides funding according to the number of students who remain and complete the classes? When students are underprepared as many are, what better way to retain them than to inflate grades? What better way to build professorial popularity than to inflate grades? What better way to gain student adulation, approbation, and stellar evaluations? This is a win-win environment: students are delighted; professors are happy; administrators are contented; even the state is satisfied.

Meanwhile, community leaders and employers are asking high school and college personnel, "Why are you graduating illiterates?" Why are you passing students from one level to another, giving them the vain assurance that they have acquired the requisite skills in language fundamentals?

Granted, there are a number of students who enter community colleges with the required skills and leave with a solid foundation. But too many others enter, move through, and leave lacking minimum language skills. Let me demonstrate. The following are segments of an essay written by a student in my **upper-level college composition class.** This student graduated from high school and, sadly, she recently received a grade of "B" in the first-year, college-level English composition class before she entered my class. After we had discussed a number of Chopin's works, I gave the students the following topic for an in-class essay: "In What Way or Ways Are Three of Chopin's Stories Similar or Different?" Here are excerpts from the essay the student wrote:

> From the written work of Chopin, each one describe in different ways. Chopin use picture mind and vivid word where she tell the readers what is happening and what is been sent. . . . Each story is characterize by a different message. . . . Patience is precious and we shouldn't destroy it by our insignificant casualty of life. . . . Babette live with her godmother who she agrees to let her visit some relatives. . . . It just happen that she would have to wait. . . . She learn the importance of have patience. . . . In conclusion, Chopin has illustrated the three stories with a suspen and message that gathers anyone's attention to summit in real life. . . .

The paper consists of three pages of writing in which practically every sentence is either ungrammatical, incoherent, or unidiomatic. The sad thought is that it has become the norm to expect papers of this caliber from students at the community college level. The seriousness of this situation speaks for itself, but I will add one reminder: **This student graduated from high school and received a "B" in freshman English in college.**

Some students argue that professors should disregard errors in grammar, syntax, and other mechanics when grading students' papers. The disturbing fact is that some professors endorse this idea, overlooking the fact that students are not saleable in the business world and are not taken seriously in the socioeconomic world without manifestation of competence in the mechanics of the English language. So where are we sending these students? Why are we sending them half-baked out of the high schools and community colleges into our communities? With state funding reduced and disbursed according to the number of students graduating from community colleges, for example, professors and administrators must still insist on the need for students to demonstrate minimum levels of competence in English language skills. On a number of occasions, I have been notified by the chairperson in my department and by the director of the Honors Program that several students "are complaining" that I teach grammar in my English and literature classes. Granted, grammar exercises are indeed outside the purview of any college curriculum; they belong at the elementary school level. However, recognizing that an ungrammatical "honors" or "college" paper is a sad oxymoron, I continue to do my small part and help as many students as I can to generate English communication skills that are truly "honors" or at least "college level."

When I was Chairperson of the English Department—College Core—at a community college in Miami, I not only encouraged the professors to teach grammar whenever they could, but I also recommended that they assign a significant number of in-class writing assignments in order to ascertain that students can demonstrate minimum competency in the English language.

This is the kind of advice I also passed on to the professors at Oakwood College—now University (Huntsville, Alabama)—when I was invited in 1994 to hold a workshop at Oakwood for the professors in the English department. The power of the word, spoken or written, cannot be overemphasized. We must send our students into the world wielding pens that are mightier than swords. And parents are very much a part of the picture. What! Do parents sometimes canvas grades on the college level and seek to apply pressure to the powers that be on behalf of their children? one may ask. The answer is yes. And, yes, sometimes they succeed. All of us—administrators, professors, staff, parents, and community leaders—must recognize that we are our students' keepers. We must realize that students with half-baked skills create half-baked communities.

Many students, victims of grade inflation, are facing difficulty, embarrassment, and failure on their jobs and in their communities. Some return disillusioned to college to populate adult literacy classes in order to acquire basic communication skills that they should have achieved before being awarded even the minimum passing grade of "C." Approximately one year ago, during the first week of classes, after checking the computer printout of all my students, I noticed that one student had already received a "B" in the freshman English composition class I was about to teach. All English professors at my college are required to do this check to ensure that students are placed in classes commensurate with their language skills. At the end of the class, I asked the student her reason for retaking the course. With resignation and an air of despair, she replied: "Dr. Charles, I had a bad experience on my job. One day, my supervisor asked me to write a report. When I took the report to her, she laughed at me and said, 'You've got to be kidding! Look at all of those errors! Go back to your desk and rewrite the report.' I rewrote the report as carefully as I could, but when I took it back to my supervisor, she sighed and said, 'I guess I'll have to write it myself.'" Naturally, the student was dismissed from the job. She said that she was retaking the class to get the basic English skills she needed. My heart went out to her. Right then and there, I determined to be her "keeper." I resolved that I would not dream of awarding her even the minimum grade of "C" unless she earned it.

I am always so very pleased when I encouonter students who know they need help and seek it. However, unfortunately, a large number of students who need remediation are convinced that they can write, especially after receiving passing grades, even "A's" in high school and college composition classes. Anyone, like me, who tells them differently is incorrect and must be upbraided. Just the other day, I advised a student to attend the writing lab and possibly enroll in a remedial English class. The student then sent me an e-mail from which I have taken the following excerpt:

> Yesterday, I was concern about your evaluation.
> I really didn't do well on that diagnostic essay
> because I didn't feel like writin. I have to assumed
> the result. I was surprise about your advised that
> I will not pass your class. . . . I consider myself as a
> competen professional. . . . Maybe your experience
> give you a idea about who is going to failure in your
> class, but is very disappointing to let down a
> student. . . . You had clip the wings of a student who
> is looking for knowledge. . . .

How many times professors like me have been charged with undermining students' self-esteem simply because we did our jobs? During the first week of each term, it is departmental policy at my college that all English professors give a diagnostic essay as a placement tool in composition classes. I had simply told the student that he MAY have difficulty in my class, basing my statement on his very poorly written diagnostic essay. But notice the irony here.

His defense clearly justifies my assessment of his writing. Notice the errors in language in his brief e-mail even though he had all the time he needed to write the e-mail **at home**. And so, the unwarranted charges continue to be hurled. Professors like me who insist on at least minimal language competency are the pariahs of academe who "clip the wings of [students] who [are] looking for knowledge." How sad!

    This student, and many others like him, fail to understand that as English professors, we have a mission—a responsibility—to "judge" their communication skills. That is what we are trained to do; that is what we are paid to do. The disturbing reality is that we are not the only ones judging our students. People in the community also expect collegiate performance from them. One thing these people definitely expect, perhaps even demand, from college students is proficiency in English language skills. Let me demonstrate. On January 3, 2003, in a real-life television courtroom scene with a popular judge, a college student was accusing the defendant—her boyfriend—of physical abuse. She was not explaining effectively how she was manhandled, though she was trying hard to do so. Suddenly, the judge said to her, "You are going to college; explain to me in plain English exactly what happened." In other words, the judge was saying: The least that we in the community are expecting from any and all college students is "plain," correct, intelligible, coherent English sentences. Is that asking too much? Of course not. But some students and professors seem disinclined to understand this reality. That day in the courtroom, the college student continued her valiant struggle with the English language. As she sought to advance her case, she said to the judge: "Your Honor, he **should not have went** to my apartment that day." I winced.

    Though there are many others, one additional incident will suffice to show that we must awake to the fact that people in our community are judging our students and are, in actuality, judging us. One day, I was listening to a radio call-in show with a famous psychologist as host. A college student called in with a problem. In a preliminary statement, the student identified the college she was attending and then proceeded to explain her dilemma.

"Did you say you are in college?" the psychologist asked.

"Yes, I am."

"You want to know why I asked," the psychologist prodded.

"Yes, I do."

"Because you said, 'He had gave me a watch for my birthday.' College students should speak correct English."

I was astounded. Never before had I heard public figures comment on incorrect English expression so forthrightly. I colored for the student, and I immediately thought of my students. Once more, it became resoundingly clear to me that we, professors, must be advised that our students are being judged in the community, and their performance can make us look good or bad. We educators must accept the fact that, in spite of the pressures to do otherwise, it is our duty to hold back our students until they have mastered basic language fundamentals.

Unfortunately, egregious errors in language surface daily in the discourse of public figures—college alumni—all around us. Television and radio college-graduate newscasters have told us repeatedly that victims are found **"laying"** on the ground. I concede that "to lie" and "to lay" often prove problematic. Therefore, I usually introduce my students early to what I call the **"chicken position,"** reminding them that adult female chickens "lay." Each term, I write the principal parts of the verbs **"to lie" and "to lay"** on the board. I explain to them the concept of transitive and intransitive verbs. Thereafter, whenever my students write or say that they were **"laying on the beach"** or that their **grandmothers were "laying on their beds,"** I would simply ask**, "Are you referring to the chicken position?"** That question would always cause laughter. I usually remind my students that **hens lay eggs; builders lay bricks, and professors are helping them to lay a foundation for their careers. But anyone in a restful or reclining position is "lying"** not **"laying."**

Additionally, I usually identify some popular incorrect expressions like **"snuck,"** emphasizing the fact that **there is no such word in the English language as "snuck."** And so, in spite of what they hear and see on television and the Internet or read in daily newspapers, they soon discover that **thieves "sneaked" in alleys, never "snuck."** The ubiquitous misuse or abuse of **"there's"** plagues television, radio, and college campuses, and abounds in every public forum, to the extent that this flagrant error is daily construed as perfect English. And so, we hear sentences like the following everyday, everywhere, even proudly spoken by those who should know better: "There's lots of issues to be discussed." "There's people who belief such and such. . . . "There's Mary, Bob, and Jane waiting in the room." I heard this from a community leader: **"There's lots of ways to get from one state to another—there's cars, there's buses, there's trains, there's planes. . . ."** Amazing! I often wonder, Are these speakers listening to what they are saying? I am constantly asking myself, Don't they know that **"there's"** (a contraction) **means "there is"**? Therefore, the grammatical expression can **never be "There is people or There is cars; never people is or cars is. . . .** Each time I hear this incorrect expression, I find myself saying audibly, sometimes silently, **"Just say 'there are'! Or use the plural contraction which is 'there're' with plural subjects."**

On community college campuses where student language skills are often sub-elementary, professors can either contribute to the problem via grade inflation or work hard to find a solution. When our students sit in our college composition classes, not knowing the difference between a noun and a verb, not to mention prepositions, conjunctions, and the rest, what are we professors to do? I am able to write the following editorial comments on my students' papers only after I have spent considerable time discussing and illustrating them: "parts of speech," "subject-verb agreement," "pronoun-antecedent agreement," "inconsistent tense," "shifts in person," "incorrect past participles," "double negatives," "double comparatives and superlatives," "active/passive voice," "fragments," and so forth. Whenever I discuss these and other syntactical structures, I am often greeted with blank stares from my students and the almost universal confession that they have no idea of what I am talking. I have since discovered that one reason some teachers do not teach these fundamentals is that they, themselves, were not taught grammar as students.

Is it any wonder, then, that I have incorporated grammar in my college English composition and even literature classes and teach it vigorously? How could I do otherwise? Indeed, drills in grammar gobble up the precious minutes that should go solely to the consolidation of ideas. Therefore, most community college professors do not teach grammar. They contend, and rightly so, that competence in grammar is a pre-college requirement. But what I cannot endorse is passing out grades based on ideas only. Regardless of how great the ideas may be, grammatical errors ruin their impact and render them unworthy of passing status. Whether we like it or not, this is the reality. I remember my elementary school days in the Caribbean when we had to analyze and parse every word in every sentence selected by our teachers.

In the typical college English composition class, when the students write many ungrammatical sentences and insist on finding out why they have received "D's" and "F's" on their papers, I often wonder what do other professors do. I mean those whose policy is never to teach grammar on the college level—specifically in English composition classes.

Let me demonstrate the dilemma. One day, my students and I were examining actual sentences taken from various anonymous essays written by their classmates. A student had written a sentence like this: *"Sometimes a person find that they are having a lot of problems as they try to keep up with their work, but you can always talk to your advisor to solve these problems."* Obviously, this student is capable of passing a basic English class as long as he understands and avoids the language errors in future papers.

"What is wrong with the change from 'a person' to 'they,'" I asked.

"Nothing!" many, actually most, answered.

"The tense is wrong," others responded with conviction, oblivious to the fact that only verbs have tense.

"And what's wrong with 'a person find,'" I continued.

"It should be 'found,'" one student proudly volunteered.

"What part of speech is 'find'? How many parts of speech are in the English language?" I asked. Blank stares! Then--

"Twelve! Six! Four!" The answers were many and incorrect. No one said eight.

"Why is the shift from 'a person' to 'you' wrong?" I pursued.

The answer came back to me in the form of a question—"Why is that wrong, Dr. Charles?" Right then, it would have been so simple if I could have replied, "Because I said so." Or, "You should have learned these language fundamentals in elementary, middle, and high school." Or, "Go to the Writing Center; they will explain it there." Or, "Go to the textbook; it will give you the answer." But what did I do? I simply rolled my sleeves up and spent the rest of that period teaching grammar. Should I have to do this? Of course not! Is it arduous? Of course! But as my students' keeper, I have no alternative. The proverbial "buck" must stop somewhere.

After we have done all that we can do to help our students improve their communication skills, when they fail to meet minimum language skills requirement, we should fail them without compunction and then square our shoulders to deflect the frigid stares and hostile glares coming from them each time we encounter them on campus. Having been bruited as the toughest professor in the English Department, I am no stranger to these glares of dislike, even contempt, and some students whom I failed (or gave a lower grade than the one expected) simply look the other way when our paths cross. Others would greet me with a victorious toss of the head the following term and announce: "I took the class again with another professor, and I received an "A." At such times, I am left speechless and incredulous. However, their grade reports often document their claim. Just yesterday, a professor informed me of a conversation she had with one of my former students in an elevator. I recalled being in the elevator with them and was told that immediately after I stepped off, the student turned to my colleague saying, "That's a mean professor! She fails eighty-five percent of her students." The professor responded, "Quite possibly they deserve to fail."

Contrary to what that student claimed, the majority of the students who remain in my classes and work steadily to the end usually pass my classes. These are the students who take my classes seriously and work with me to improve their communication skills. I encounter them regularly: in neighborhood banks, in drug stores, department stores, in supermarkets, and elsewhere. Many of them would detain me for a chat, thanking me profusely for equipping them with language skills that brought them success in their various careers. With one voice, they would say, "You were tough, but we learned so much!" It is difficult to express the gratification I experience when I receive unsolicited letters like the one I have included on page 73 to demonstrate that students often understand or respect so-called "toughness" and appreciate professors who help them to acquire knowledge. I have decided to omit the student's name.

    I'll never forget one Saturday evening as my husband and I strolled the aisles of a neighborhood drug store, a middle-aged woman kept us talking for no less than fifteen minutes. She recalled scenes in a class she had taken with me a few years ago. She praised my teaching style and spoke with pride of the "vast" (her word) knowledge she had acquired in my class. Her parting words to my husband were, "Take care of her. She insisted on excellence without compromise, and that has made the difference for me and her other students." When I am inclined to despair, words like these buoy me up and remind me that I am my students' keeper. When I see and hear of my students' successes, I know that my "toughness" has paid off. One of my former students wrote to me in 1995 as she was about to enter Wellesley. Here is an excerpt from her letter:

> You put your whole body and soul into teaching our class and showed us what writers we could become if we really made the effort. You took us beyond ourselves, and impressing you with my <u>Wuthering Heights</u> paper was one of my greatest pleasures.

What delightful words! I have received many notes and letters of this tenor, but reference to one or two other letters is sufficient to demonstrate that students appreciate those who set standards for them. They often see us, professors, as role models who enable them to achieve the goals we have achieved. Here are segments of a letter that came to me in 1994 from a former student residing in Hawaii:

> I am taking graduate classes at the University of Hawaii. . . . I also have a part-time job as a teacher/tutor to pregnant teens. . . . I learned so much from your classes. After I receive my Masters and Ph.D.

degrees, like you, I am interested in teaching at a community college, also like you. . . .

What pride we feel when our students inform us that we have helped them to achieve goals they have set for themselves.

My students' successes encourage me to press on and wade through stacks and stacks of papers riddled with errors in grammar and mechanics. How can papers be labeled "college level" if almost every other word has to be circled and marked "incorrect"? But this is what college professors like me must encounter. *Since this language deficit is our reality, in all disciplines across the curriculum, our duty is to keep our students in our classes until they are able to demonstrate that they have acquired minimum language skills. And when it is obvious that college-level performance is impossible, we should refer our students to remedial classes. One means of ascertaining the students' acquisition of fundamental language skills is to assign in-class essays. I would recommend that at least sixty percent of all brief essays be written in class where students must cultivate and rely on their individual skills instead of the input of others.*

Chief among the words of advice that I proffer to my fellow educators is that we resolve to resist the built-in pressures in our education system that come from all sources—from students, parents, colleagues, administrators, or elsewhere—to award even minimum passing grades to students who have not grasped the fundamentals of the English language. Students must learn to communicate and read with comprehension, since these basic skills undergird success in social, political, economic, financial, and practically every other interaction. We must say "no" to our students when they push for undeserved grades.

At a community college with many committees to serve on, projects to embark upon, and long on-campus hours to observe, at what price are we professors asked to fit into the Procrustean bed of demands from students, administrators, and even parents? At what price are we asked to "keep" or retain our students when a significant number of them withdraw from our classes as soon as it becomes clear that a grade of "A," "B," or even "C" must be earned and not acquired as a gift? At what price must I be the keeper of my students when, at the drop of a hat, a number of them are in the chairperson's office (or even the dean's) threatening to drop my class, complaining that I am teaching grammar, that I am too demanding, that I am too tough? And yet, my daily effort to help my students achieve academic equilibrium is, unquestionably, the biggest contribution I can make to the mission of my college.

    At the end of each day on campus, my hands are white; my clothes are white; chalk is everywhere; I am exhausted, but I know I have made a difference in the lives of my students. Did I say end? Let's not forget the seemingly unending hours we English professors invest at home each day, grading stacks of papers, often until the wee hours of each morning. Somehow, we educators, whether in the school system or on college campuses, are the collective "keepers" of our students in their rites of passage. In the relay of responsibility from K through 12 through community college, we must insist that students work for the grades they receive and help them acquire true self-esteem. I am hoping that one day, "honors student," "highschool graduate," and "college graduate" will no longer be misnomers as they often are today. I am striving to have my students experience the pride that accompanies true achievement.

A STUDENT SAYS THANK YOU

January 17, 1992

Dr Delpha CHARLES - Language Arts Professor
MIAMI-DADE COMMUNITY COLLEGE
300 NE 2d Avenue
Miami, FL 33132

Dear Dr CHARLES:

I wish for you to know how significant an impact you have made on me - an effect which extends far beyond the mere tutelage of English Composition mechanics.

It has not been easy to return to school at age forty, and as you know I was initially quite intimidated by the grammatical skills my classmates demonstrated. I gauged that were I to accept my shortcomings and tough it out through the early exercises, a truly intriguing educational experience would be in the offing. I was to be rewarded far beyond my expectations.

The diversity at MDCC is fascinating - the scope of which was particularly apparent in your ENC 1101 class; I was captivated by the way you addressed the various needs and abilities of such a broad cross-section of humanity. I gained a deep respect for your profession as a whole by observing how difficult it has become to meet the needs of today's dynamic society.

One so seldom encounters professional excellence and commitment in this day and age that I felt compelled to organize and articulate my appreciation for your having imbued in me a respect for learning - as well as finding the time to encourage my writing by your thoughtful, comprehensive, and exhaustive critiques of my class work.

I will not soon forget our inspiring talks - they have proven to be the impetus for seminal change in this particular student - and while I have occasionally expressed it, I feel it important that I restate these sentiments in a more tangible medium.

Thank-you.

I will never forget the day I successfully defended my dissertation at the University of Miami and was greeted, by the chairman of my doctoral committee, in these immortal words, "Congratulations, Dr. Charles!" As he ushered me back into the room to face the august group of professors who had just interrogated me, I remember thinking, Am I worthy to share this lofty title with the intellectual giants seated here? I had so recently responded to every conceivable question they had pelted at me to test my scholastic mettle, and like Babe Ruth in rare form, I had thrown every answer back at them with finesse and confidence, to the extent that they returned the same awe with which I had viewed them throughout the years. In that room, as in the case with Elijah and Elisha, the mantle was passed to me, but I felt unworthy. The title "Doctor" hung loosely on me as Shakespeare says of Macbeth's new title, but the invigorating thrill of success permeated my being.

I have no apology for anyone who objects to my emphasis on excellence. I will not ask my students to forgive me as I seek to fortify them with the skills that will enable them to achieve success as executives, political leaders, doctors, lawyers, educators, business personnel, and other valuable contributors in our community. Some day, I will be passing my mantle to my students. The ones who have endured will take it and wear it proudly, and they will assure me in words or demeanor: **"You were our keeper, and you have kept us well."**

6. IS WAR A NECESSARY EVIL?

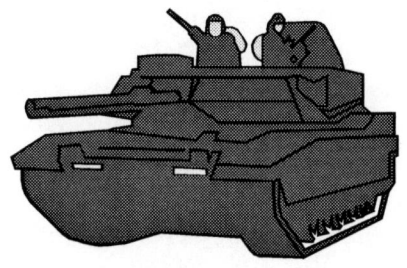

INTRODUCTION

Even in waging war, cherish the spirit of peacemaker; that, by conquering those whom you attack, you may lead them back to the advantages of peace.

Saint Augustine

Inherent in the above words of Saint Augustine is the looming paradox of warfare. Though war lays waste and is therefore abhorrent, when it is fought for a worthy cause, is it justifiable? Is there ever a worthy cause for warfare? When a war is fought to a conclusion and is then followed by peace and reconstruction, can it be deemed creator as well as destroyer? In other words, does warfare have any trace of good? Many would respond with a resounding negative. It is

June 2011. Our nation is at war. Most of us lament and ask, why? On September 11, 2001, America was attacked by terrorists. In our anguish, we asked and continue to ask, "Why?" Why do human beings wage war? Is there no other way to resolve conflicts? Each week we agonize as we watch on ABC the names of our brave, young men and women, all heroes, killed in Iraq and Afghanistan. We weep for them and their families, and we continue to ask, why?

Who likes war? No one. Perhaps not even the people who seem to relish it. And yet, we must face the realization that warfare is endemic to the human condition. Prehistoric man battled his neighbors. Within families and sub-segments of the earliest communities, there was internecine warfare when individual rights were violated. But let's go much farther back. There was warfare in the Garden of Eden. The serpent conquered Adam and Eve. Actually, let's not stop there. Let's go even farther back and try to come to terms with the fact that warfare had its inception in heaven:

> And there was war in heaven: Michael and his angels fought against the dragon [the devil]; and the dragon fought and his angels, and prevailed not; neither was their place found any more in heaven. And the great dragon was cast out, that old serpent, called the Devil, and Satan, which deceiveth the whole world: he was cast out into the earth, and his angels were cast out with him. . . . Woe to the inhabiters of the earth and of the sea! for the devil is come down unto you, having great wrath, because he knoweth that he hath but a short time.
>
> (Revelation 12: 7-12)

The universality of warfare is a rude awakening indeed. Here's the bleak reality: there will always be conflict in our human experience. There will continue to be a seismic clash between the forces of good and evil until mankind vacates this planet. Not until the ultimate battle—Armageddon—will evil be destroyed. Only then will pain and suffering, death and destruction, and warfare cease. How we long for that day!

Some wars are defensive, some preemptive, some retaliatory, some rapacious, and some simply contentious and downright unnecessary. The idea that many, perhaps most, wars are unnecessary is effectively portrayed in Jonathan Swift's immortal satire, *Gulliver's Travels* (1726).

This book is predominantly perceived as an innocent children's storybook. It is anything but. Swift angrily chastises the rulers of his eighteenth-century world (specifically Europe) and satirically knocks their collective heads together while he seeks to demonstrate that most wars are the consequence of irrational, petulant, childish behavior often triggered by egocentrism and overweening hubris. In this book, Lemuel Gulliver, an English doctor, is shipwrecked on the island of Lilliput. After lying unconscious on the beach for some time, he awakes to the realization that he is surrounded by a crowd of curious little people, each one no taller than approximately six inches. This giant (to them he is) is immobilized—tied up—and totally at the mercy of these tiny people. The king of Lilliput has to climb a ladder in order to access Gulliver's ear and interrogate this monstrosity that has washed up on his shore.

The tiny king imperiously plies Gulliver with questions about the country he has left behind. After listening to Gulliver, the little king is loud in his condemnation of Gulliver's compatriots, denouncing the many wars they have fought. He is outraged to hear that Gulliver's countrymen could be so inhuman, so barbaric, as to shed the blood of their fellowmen with little cause. However, ironically, during Gulliver's brief stay in Lilliput, war breaks out. Gulliver soon discovers that the Lilliputians are just as gratuitously warlike as the Europeans. Thousands die, and blood flows in the streets of Lilliput simply because half of the population believe that, as one prepares breakfast, eggs should be broken at the big end, while the other half insist that the little end is more practical. After watching the Big Endians and Little Endians destroy one another, Gulliver leaves Lilliput despondent, recognizing that, in their neighborhoods, in their streets, in their cities and countries, human beings don't hesitate to kill one another over trifles. Another dominant message in Swift's satire is that quite often, intellectual giants (symbolized by Gulliver) allow themselves to be rendered impotent while mental dwarfs take administrative control.

Without doubt, we would agree that judicious leaders would avoid warfare except when they are compelled to fight defensively to repel attack and preserve life. For example, in 1415, the valiant King Henry V of England engaged in a war he deemed justifiable. Shakespeare portrays him charismatic and brave in the famous Battle of Agincourt, as he motivates and energizes his soldiers. Overwhelmed by the enormity of the imminent battle against the French, he does not fail to appeal to a Higher Force to help his soldiers gain victory: "O God of battles, steel my soldiers' hearts!" he implores. History informs us that his prayer was answered in a decisive victory.

Edson Buntin, like Shakespeare, decries warfare but submits that it is often inescapable and sometimes necessary to bolster an empire for the common good. In his book titled *Anu Bantu: Treasure Isle and Haunted Park*, he explains:

> Imperialism has its good as well as its bad. Moreover, it cannot be avoided. When two nations meet, the weaker will inevitably be a colony of the stronger economically, culturally or militarily. Besides, there's no development of civilisation without imperialism. The history of man's development proceeds as follows: first the family, then the tribe, then the city, then the state or nation and finally the Empire. . . . Within the Empire, everyone was compelled to obey the Emperor, so there was peace. Of course there were good Empires

and bad Empires. (286)

For further clarification, Buntin gives some excellent examples of the beneficial impact of certain empires which waged warfare to effect peace. For example:

> At about 100 B.C. in the Mediterranean area, no one could send a package or letter from Egypt, Judea, Syria, Greece, or Asia Minor and know it would arrive in Rome. Nothing could travel safely in this region because of the vicious and savage piracy. Pirates would destroy ships, murder travelers, and take their possessions as booty. But when the Roman Empire took control, the Romans gave Pompey a massive army to sweep the Mediterranean Sea clean of piracy. This he did most effectively, and safe travel and communication were restored. (287)

The quotes in this chapter are a few samples among the compendium of ideas Shakespeare has expressed concerning warfare. His overriding sentiment is the senselessness and the tragedy of warfare, though he admits it must be fought bravely when life is at stake and there is no other option; in other words, when there is a worthy cause.

I See the Imminent Death

I see
The imminent death of twenty thousand men
That for a fantasy and trick of fame
Go to their graves like beds, fight for a plot
Whereon the numbers cannot try the cause,
Which is not tomb enough and continent
To hide the slain.
(*Hamlet* 4. 4. 59-65)

PARAPHRASE

I recognize that in a short while, twenty thousand men will die. These are men who deluded themselves by thinking that becoming soldiers would bring them fame or renown. And so, they go to their graves as if they were beds, and they fight on a piece of land that is so small that there isn't room enough for all the soldiers nor does it provide enough space to entomb their bodies.

O War, Thou Son of Hell

      O War, thou son of Hell,
Whom angry Heavens do make their minister,
Throw in the frozen bosoms of our part
Hot coals of vengeance! Let no soldier fly.
He that is truly dedicate to war
Hath no self-love, nor he that loves himself
Hath not essentially but by circumstance
The name of valor.
(2 *Henry VI* 5. 2. 33-39)

PARAPHRASE

O war, you are an offspring of hell. In righteous indignation, the heavenly beings use you as their messenger to dole out retribution. Fill the cold, cowardly hearts of our men (our soldiers) with fiery vengeance! Don't let any of them desert. The soldier who is seriously committed to warfare does not seek to spare himself, and the one who seeks to preserve himself is not truly brave, though at any given time he may be presumed so.

Once More Unto the Breach

Once more unto the breach, dear friends, once more,
Or close the wall up with our English dead.
In peace there's nothing so becomes a man
As modest stillness and humility.
But when the blast of war blows in our ears,
Then imitate the action of the tiger,
Stiffen the sinews, summon up the blood,
Disguise fair nature with hard-favored rage.
Then lend the eye a terrible aspect,
Let it pry through the portage of the head
Like the brass cannon. Let the brow o'erwhelm it
As fearfully as doth a galled rock
O'erhang and jutty his confounded base,
Swilled with the wild and wasteful ocean.
Now set the teeth and stretch the nostril wide,
Hold hard the breath, and bend up every spirit
To his full height. On, on, you noblest English,
Whose blood is fet from fathers of war proof!
Fathers that, like so many Alexanders,
Have in these parts from morn till even fought,
And sheathed their swords for lack of argument.
Dishonor not your mothers. Now attest
That those whom you called fathers did beget you.
Be copy now to men of grosser blood,
And teach them how to war. And you, good yeomen,
Whose limbs were made in England, show us here
The mettle of your pasture. Let us swear
That you are worth your breeding, which I doubt not,
For there is none of you so mean and base
That hath not noble luster in your eyes.
I see you stand like greyhounds in the slips,
Straining upon the start. The game's afoot.
Follow your spirit, and upon this charge
Cry "God for Harry, England, and Saint George!"
(*Henry V* 3. 1. 1-34)

Delpha Charles, Ph.D.

No longer a carefree youth, Prince Hal is now King Henry V, and he is exhorting his soldiers in the Battle of Agincourt.

PARAPHRASE

My soldiers, my dear friends, let us go forward once again. Let us resume the onslaught at the battle front, or else we might as well use the corpses of our English soldiers to reinforce or repair the wall that separates our army from our enemies (the French). In peaceful times, nothing is more manly than unassuming quietness and meekness. However, when we hear the resounding trumpet that heralds warfare, we should use the tiger's demeanor as a model. We should harden the tendons and let our blood boil, masking our mild countenance with grim-faced ferocity. Then develop a fierce look or glare in the eye that penetrates the opening in the head like a cannon ball made of brass. Let the eyebrow protrude over the eye, as menacing as a rock that has been gutted by the sea—a rock drenched and wasted by the boisterous ocean. Now clench your teeth and flare your nostrils. Hold your breath tightly and summon up your courage to the fullest extent. Those among you who are members of the aristocracy, born of English warrior stock, go forward. Your fathers have all fought in this territory from morning until evening like Alexander the Great, and they put away their swords only when there was no more reason to fight. Do not disgrace your mothers. Now is the time to prove that the men you called fathers did indeed conceive you. Be examples for men who are lesser born, and show them how to be good warriors. And you strong, dependable men from England's rural areas, show us your grit, your sturdy character. Let us be able to verify your solid, robust upbringing which I don't doubt that you possess, because not one of you is of such a low rank or inferior stock that you do not have an air of dignity about you. I watch you standing here like greyhounds, restrained by collars, lunging forward, eager to start the race. The game has started. Keep up your high-spirited momentum, and as you leap forward, shout "God bless King Henry, England, and Saint George!"

Farewell the Plume`d Troop

Farewell the plume`d troop and the big wars
That make ambition virtue! Oh, farewell,
Farewell the neighing steed and the shrill trump,
The spirit-stirring drum, the ear-piercing fife,
The royal banner and all quality,
Pride, pomp, and circumstance of glorious war!
And, O you mortal engines, whose rude throats
The immortal Jove's dread clamors counterfeit,
Farewell! Othello's occupation's gone!
(*Othello* 3. 3. 349-57)

War does have an element of shock and awe, but is the loss of lives worth it? Many like Othello would like to say "farewell" to all aspects of warfare.

PARAPHRASE

Goodbye to soldiers wearing large feathers in their helmets, and goodbye to elaborate warfare that causes vainglorious pride to be viewed as virtuous or honorable! Oh, goodbye to the neighing horses, the piercing trumpets, the rousing drums, the deafening fifes, the royal flag, and all military rank. Goodbye to all dignity, splendor, and pageantry of grandiose warfare! And goodbye you deadly cannons whose boisterous throats emit the deafening sounds that imitate the noisy, horrific thunder of immortal Jove. Goodbye! Othello has abandoned his military career.

What Would You Have Me Do?

What would you have me do? Go to the wars, would you? Where a man may serve seven years for the loss of a leg, and have not money enough in the end to buy him a wooden one?
(*Pericles* 4. 6. 180-84)

In his works, Shakespeare honestly assesses war, obviously concluding that it may be necessary in some circumstances, but because of its devastating consequences, it should be avoided whenever possible.

PARAPHRASE

What would you suggest that I do? Enlist in the armed forces and go to war, although a man may serve his country for seven years only to suffer the loss of a leg as a consequence? What's more, he may not even have enough money to purchase a wooden leg in the long run.

COMMENTARY: The Paradox of Warfare: Destroyer or Creator?

War is, indeed, a paradox. It is an instrument of chaos, and yet it imposes order on chaos. It lays waste, and yet it builds. It destroys communities, and yet it establishes empires. It creates wilderness and devastation, and yet it is an instrument of civilization. It is detested by all (at least by most), and yet it has been a frequent occurrence, a way of life, from the inception of planet earth. This is the war imperative—a constant from the dawn of man's history.

So what is this war imperative that characterizes the human experience? In peaceful times, it lurks on the horizon. But here's the irony. Even as war destroys, it often lays the foundation for peace and rebirth. In 1776, it was warfare that hammered out the peaceful existence that we now enjoy in America. It was warfare that imposed order on the chaotic environs of the Arabian Desert and blazed a trail to civilization over four thousand years before Christ was born. Thousands of years later, it was warfare that tamed our western land mass and prepared the way for the establishment of our civilized communities similar to those that already existed in the ancient eastern world. In other words, it is warfare and empire building that engendered the possibility of the globalization we now enjoy. Edson Buntin effectively emphasizes this beneficial global unity that resulted from empire building. He declares:

> Without empires mankind would still be living in some isolated tribes, in xenophobic villages or city states. It's the Empires that dispersed the cultures of earth's peoples all around the world. Out of this evolved one global Ethos. . . . In our modern world this global multiplex is linked and held together by the aeroplane, the internet, the mobile phone, and all the other gadgets from our revolution in communication. These gadgets bring the global culture to the realm of every city, nation, tribe and people; so the world has now become one global village enjoying common pleasures but also plagued with common woes like unfair trade and global warming. Moreover all the actions of one nation now impact on all the others. We are all now bound together in one great unbreakable and inescapable concatenation. That is what we call globalisation.. It's like a world empire led by the United Nations. It makes each man his brother's Keeper, as the people of the world are forced to share objectives and experiences. It brings mankind together in one culture and in global unity. It is a good thing for humanity. (293-95)

To sum up definitively, let me reiterate a few facts about the war imperative and the paradox of warfare in the following paragraphs.

From the cradle of civilization, from early Mesopotamia—land between and around the three great rivers: Euphrates, Tigris, and Nile (the Fertile Crescent)—there has been warfare. And it never ends. From 4000 B.C. when the Sumerians (the earliest known people of Mesopotamia) established themselves in small city-states, each with its own ruler, there was warfare as the rulers jostled one another for control of land and water.

They built large, elaborate pyramid-temples called ziggurats, and the leading families and officials lived in magnificent palaces with spacious courtyards. Warfare became a way of life, a means of survival. The warriors dominated the scene because their communities depended on them for protection; consequently, they often became hereditary rulers. Invasion and conquest are indigenous to the history of the ancient Middle East. Repeatedly, bands of nomads and fierce warriors plundered the rich cities of the Fertile Crescent. Many of these invaders looted, burned, and moved on, but others established themselves as rulers of the conquered territory. They often built elaborate, well-organized, peaceful empires.

Around 3150 B.C. in eastern North Africa—in the vicinity of the Nile River—ancient Egyptian civilization was established under the Pharaohs until approximately 31 B.C. when Rome conquered Egypt and made it a province. For thousands of years, Egyptian military forces kept invading tribes at bay. The Pharaohs irrigated the Nile Valley, and agriculture flourished as a consequence. They built elaborate structures including the famous pyramids which were tombs for the Pharaohs. By engaging and repelling rival forces, the Pharaohs were able to establish long periods of peace and unity among the Egyptian people, and Egypt's wealth increased significantly. After Tutankhamun and two other kings died, the military strong man Ramses I became king. His grandson Ramses II continued to build the Egyptian nation, fought foreign powers that threatened, and sought to maintain peace.

Around 2300 B.C. Sargon of Akkad emerged as a pioneer in early civilization, since he conquered Sumer and built the first empire known in history. Warfare was the instrument that changed the political landscape of the earliest civilizations, as one powerful dynasty gave way to another. And so, after many years, the resourceful Sumerian empire under Sargon was toppled, and various other conquerors settled in Sumer until around 1790 B.C. when the powerful Babylonians under Hammurabi conquered and occupied the region. King Hammurabi built up an impressive empire and established laws and customs known as the Code of Hammurabi—the first significant collection of laws in history.

Warfare and plunder continued throughout the years as the area was dominated by the Hittites and then the fierce, terrifying Assyrians. The Assyrian army plundered, burned pillaged, massacred, took captive slaves, and terrorized the area until 612 B.C. when the Assyrian empire was overthrown by joint forces in the region. The powerful Babylonian empire then emerged under the mighty King Nebuchadnezzar whose kingdom occupied territory from the Persian Gulf to the Mediterranean Sea. He restructured and repaired the temples, canals, irrigation system, and palaces of Babylon. On the steps of a large ziggurat, he constructed the famous Hanging Gardens of Babylon, one of the Wonders of the ancient world.

Cyrus the Great, King of Persia, overthrew the Babylonian Empire in 539 B.C. and established the largest empire in the ancient world. The Persian Empire expanded for approximately 3,000 miles and flourished for 200 years. The Persians allowed the captured people to continue their customs and religious practices. The Persian Emperor Darius built the most powerful and extensive empire in the region. During his reign—522 B.C. to 486 B.C.—he established laws and order. He constructed or repaired hundreds of miles of roads and boosted trade by instituting the use of weights and measures and coins. He built a prosperous, peaceful nation.

Those who decry warfare must agree that defensive warfare is often necessary. Often, warfare is the only instrument of survival, the only means of establishing or maintaining peace, stability, normalcy and well being. In the rest of this chapter, a few historical references will suffice to demonstrate that warfare is often the paradoxical instrument of peace.

Some time around A.D. 449, three Germanic tribes arrived in Britain ostensibly to help the Britons repel the murderous bands of Picts and Scots who descended on them from the North. Since Britain was part of the Roman Empire at that time, the Britons or Celts appealed to Rome to help them resist the invaders, but Rome had its own internal problems; hence no help was extended to the British who had no alternative but to invite the warrior tribes from the Scandinavian Peninsula as mercenaries to help them survive. The three Germanic tribes that arrived in Britain—the Angles, the Saxons, and the Jutes—made short work of the Picts and Scots. Thereafter, an agreement was made whereby the warriors were given a portion of land and payment in exchange for protection, security, and peaceful living. However, these fierce Germanic predators construed the Britons' emphasis on peace as cowardice. They saw fertile land, clement weather, and people incapable or unwilling to fight effectively. Consequently, in a relatively short time, a reign of terror ensued. The Germanic warriors slaughtered the Britons—men, women, and children—and eventually seized the land. The land that the Angles occupied was called Angle Land ("Engle Land" and eventually "England" emerged as a derivative).

Over four hundred years later, unlike the Celts (Britons) who were decimated because they did not or could not fight, the now established Angles and Saxons valiantly repelled the marauding Vikings. It was then the Anglo Saxons' turn to fight heroically and unflinchingly for their own survival. In European history, the eighth to tenth century A.D. is often referred to as the Viking Age because during that period, the Vikings or Danes (also Scandinavian warriors) ravaged the coast of England and the rest of Europe in their impressively built ships.

But England was spared destruction because of the advent of an Anglo Saxon king, himself a great warrior: Alfred the Great, King of Wessex, became the first king of England in A.D. 871. He was a mighty king, indeed, doing all he could to maintain peace and stability in an effort to build the English nation. **He recognized that in order to preserve peace, he had to fight to keep the Vikings at bay.** Consequently, he organized a substantial army. He built new forts and strengthened old ones. He assembled a navy and built sturdy ships to transport his soldiers who engaged the Vikings before they reached the English shores.

As a social reformer, King Alfred was no less brilliant. He recognized that an educated populace was a *sine qua non* to build a nation. He therefore built schools, supplying them with books and other facilities. He established towns and instituted a legal and penal system. He promoted Christianity and was instrumental in the conversion of many Anglo Saxons (pagans) to Christianity. Having learned Latin, he had segments of the Bible translated to the English vernacular, and he attached these Biblical passages to the pews in the churches he had built. The English nation grew and flourished during the reign of the great King Alfred.

Of course, four American-Mexican Indian communities—the Mayans, the Toltecs, the Aztecs, and the Incas—also burgeoned into powerful empires after warfare led to eventual peace. The Mayans, for example, occupied a vast territory in central Mexico from the fourth to the sixteenth century. During that time, they engaged in raids, pillaging, many battles, and even human sacrifice. However, throughout the years, powerful Mayan leaders built strong, peaceful, civilized communities. They recorded their communal exploits in hieroglyphic sculptures; they built pyramids and monumental temples. In addition to their impressive architecture, other Mayan achievements were an advanced knowledge of mathematics and astronomy and a highly accurate calendar.

And what about China and the Mongolian Empire? We have heard of Genghis Khan (1162-1227), the ruthless marauder, the pillager, the relentless invader, the barbarian, but how many of us are aware that he has been considered the greatest empire builder in history, bar none? This man called Temujin renamed himself Genghis Khan (Supreme Emperor) and earned the title indeed in that he united all the tribes in Mongolia to build one large stabilized nation. No one before him even came close to building a world empire. As general of the Mongol army, even as Genghis Khan ravaged the civilized world, he transformed warfare into an instrument of intercontinental unification. In eastern Asia, the Mongols (Genghis Khan and his sons and grandsons) created the unified and powerful nation of China by merging a number of conquered territories. They also formed one large Russian nation by uniting a number of Slavic city-states. Additionally, they created countries like India and Korea.

One of the greatest achievements of Genghis Khan is that he opened a path of commerce, trade, and diplomacy from the East to the West. At the time of his birth, the eastern and western civilizations had little or no knowledge of any other communities beyond their own. For example, no one in Europe had heard of a country called China, nor did anyone in China know of the existence of Europe. Because of the Mongols, European traders and merchants as well as explorers like the Italian Marco Polo had access and safe travel to the massive wealth of the East—its treasures, its silks and other clothing, its spices, its art forms, its technology, and its culture in general. This link to the East laid the foundation for the Renaissance in Europe, creating a transition from medieval to modern times.

Little wonder, therefore, that even in an opium-induced sleep, Samuel Taylor Coleridge was still seemingly captivated, mesmerized by the vision he had formed after reading Marco Polo's description of Kublai Khan's luxurious palace which he (Polo) had visited. Coleridge's poem has immortalized an impressive view of Khan's palace, and so we get a glimpse, or at least an idea, of the lavish wealth and vastness of the Chinese Empire—the Mongol Dynasty—created by Kublai Khan (grandson of Genghis Khan). The poetic fragment titled "Kubla Khan" (1798) describes Kublai Khan's palace in his summer capitol which was called Xanadu. Coleridge seems to be saying, come and observe in awe with me:

> In Xanadu did Kubla Khan
> A stately pleasure-dome decree:
> Where Alph, the sacred river, ran
> Through caverns measureless to man
>   Down to a sunless sea.
> So twice five miles of fertile ground
> With walls and towers were girdled round:
> And there were gardens bright with sin-
> uous rills,
> Where blossomed many an incense-bearing
>   tree;
> And here were forests ancient as the
>   hills,
> Enfolding sunny spots of greenery.
> ....

Conquest has always been the primary instrument for building empire. Though their achievements cannot be compared with those of the Mongols, perhaps no other community in history has emphasized so unrelentingly the importance of warfare as did the Spartans. These were tough, rugged, indomitable inhabitants of the ancient city-state of Sparta. The welfare of the state was the focal point of their lives. To men, women, and children, nothing was more important than maintenance of the status quo and normalcy of Sparta. Children belonged not to their parents but to the state. At the age of seven, every healthy Spartan boy was sent to military school where he learned to endure severe pain. Sickly children were exposed and left to die. After many years of training, the healthy Spartan male became a soldier. His sole duty was to fight to the death for the preservation of his state. Spartan mothers were pleased and proud to have their sons die in battle, as long as they could be assured that their sons fought to their deaths to defend Sparta. The most peace-loving person could quite possibly admire, or at least respect, the granite courage of the Spartans whose way of life may be viewed as a metaphor for the war imperative.

The Spartan collective and unyielding belief that the state had to be preserved and protected with each soldier's last breath is documented in the famous Battle of Thermopylae (480 B.C.) when three hundred heroic Spartans fought valiantly to the last man against the mighty Persian army (over ten thousand strong). Though all three hundred Spartans died that day, they were victorious in that they unflinchingly engaged the Persians long enough to allow the rest of the Greek army to retreat safely.

Like the Spartans, the Athenian soldier Phidippides may have willingly given up his life for the benefit of the state when he ran over twenty-six miles from Marathon to Athens to proclaim the good news that the Athenians had defeated the Persians (Battle of Marathon 490 B.C.).

Immediately after he announced victory, he dropped dead, but he had achieved his purpose. The word "marathon" came into our language—and the marathon was included in the Olympic games—because of this remarkable incident. And rightly so.

It is rewarding to recognize that in the same way a small body of soldiers at Thermopylae saved the Greeks, just so the small island of Antigua played a significant supporting role to England in the seventeenth, eighteenth, and nineteenth centuries when England was embroiled in warfare to preserve the large empire she had built. Antigua's topographical outlay made it an ideal British military base. At various strategic points around the island are vestiges of the historical sites used by the British in the colonial era, most of them now tourist attractions. For example, Monk's Hill was the site of a large fort (1689) built to defend Falmouth, Antigua's first town and harbour, from the French. Nelson's Dockyard at English Harbour was a pivotal naval rest and maintenance stop for British war ships. The famous British hero Lord Horatio Nelson was in command here in 1784 and later. Hence, the dockyard was named after him. The fort at Shirley Heights was a military complex and look out post strategically located on a hill a short distance from the Dockyard. The Royal Artillery Gunner's Barracks were located here.

Another fortress and look out post of much significance in Antigua was Fort James established when St. John's town became larger than Falmouth and Parham about 1703. There were around ten cannons at this fort. It is said that it took eleven men to handle one cannon which weighed two and a half tons. These cannons continue to be quite an attraction for the tourists who continually visit the fort. Even now, I can recall the many occasions on which I enjoyed the invigorating waters of the beach at Fort James during my adolescent years. It was customary for many residents of St. John's during the early years to bicycle or walk to Fort

James for an exhilarating dip in the refreshing water of the Atlantic Ocean before going to work. Each time I revisit Antigua, I am reminded of the vital contribution it made to Britain's military effort during the colonial years.

    War is, indeed, an inescapable part of this life. As we interact with others on planet earth, we strive for peace but often must wage war. When missiles are hurled at us, for some time, we may run for cover. But when our space is invaded, and our very lives are threatened, we must fight for survival. In any community, where hooligans attack innocents and seek to usurp the peace, battles must be fought. However, a point frequently overlooked, but one which must be stressed, is that in our daily interaction at home or abroad, warfare does not have to include violence. Violence is not endemic to warfare. We can wage war with our wits. We can wage war with our words. We can make our pens or word processors mightier than swords. We can even wage war with our silence. There is psychological as well as diplomatic warfare. Any nonviolent method that works is best. But when there is no pacific solution possible, then we must take up our swords and fight as courageous warriors for peace.

7. RELIGION

INTRODUCTION

According to the parish register of the Stratford-on-Avon Church, the infant William Shakespeare was baptized on April 26, 1564. His father, John Shakespeare, was a landowner and a leading citizen of Stratford. His mother, Mary Arden, was a Roman Catholic, and though his father also attended the Stratford Church, he did so intermittently. The parish register indicates that the Stratford Church featured in certain other significant incidents in Shakespeare's life including his marriage to Anne Hathawey, his children's baptism, and his death on April 23, 1616. However, we have no detailed information regarding any of these events beyond the journal entries in the Stratford Register.

Little is known of Shakespeare's life in general, and of his religious life, we know even less. We can then only deduce or extrapolate his attitude, his philosophy, regarding church attendance and religious matters from the statements he has permitted his characters to express. One or two such statements appear later in this chapter.

The Advent Message Comes to Montserrat

As I searched for information regarding Shakespeare's church affiliation, my mind wandered back to my religious upbringing in the Caribbean, and many significant circumstances surrounding my childhood church flooded my mind spontaneously. I had a church-centered childhood in the island of Montserrat. I was born a Seventh-day Adventist, and as such, my life was different from those of many of my friends. I remember my parents' emphasis on healthy foods and habits: no pork or unhealthy meat; no alcohol; no smoking. These were strict rules of my church, and my parents observed them stringently. I can envision once more my mother gathering my siblings and me around her every Friday at sunset to welcome the Sabbath. We would sing hymns and read passages from the Bible and prepare ourselves for church the following day.

Yes, each Saturday was a very special day in our lives. It was a day reserved for rest and church attendance. Even as I write, I recall that it was my mother who was primarily responsible for the establishment of the Seventh-day Adventist Church in the island of Montserrat. I remember the circumstance as she told it to us. She was eleven years old at the time. On one special day in my mother's life, anyone listening would quite possibly have heard a conversation like this one between my mother (Elizabeth) and my grandmother:

Grandmother:	Elizabeth, where have you been? I have been calling you for the past half an hour. The dishes should have been washed long ago.
Mother:	I'm sorry Mamma. I'll do them right away.
Grandmother:	You have disappeared a number of times this week. What are you up to?
Mother:	There's something I have to tell you and Dadda. A strange man has been coming every afternoon to speak to the people sitting in front of Mr. Walker's store. The people usually stop what they are doing and listen to him. You and Dadda need to hear what he has to say. He is telling us some very important things about the Bible, things I've never heard before. You need to hear him.
Grandmother:	I'm very busy right now. What is he saying?
Mother:	Well, he's telling us that Saturday is the Sabbath that God says to keep holy in the Commandments (Exodus 20), not Sunday. He says that Saturday is a special day that is discussed throughout the Bible. That's the day that Jesus and his disciples and the apostles went to church. The synagogue or temple is what they

called church back then. You need to hear what the man is saying.

Like most churchgoers on the island, my grandparents were staunch Anglicans. My grandfather was actually an Anglican preacher. Therefore, at first, my grandparents ignored my mother. However, she insisted each day, "You must come with me and listen to that man. You must hear all of the important things he is saying."

Finally, after much coaxing, one day my grandparents accompanied my mother to the central spot in the village—the area in front of Mr. Walker's grocery store. There he was, the evangelist that my mother had described. Armed with his Bible, he was speaking to a relatively large crowd, quoting text after text to document or verify all that he was saying. For example, he read passages in *Genesis* that indicate that during creation week, God rested from all work on Saturday and blessed that day (*Genesis* 2: 2, 3). He reminded the people that, as Moses led the Israelites from Egypt, God sent a double portion of manna on Fridays so that none would have to be gathered on Saturdays, the day of rest and worship. And actually when some people went out to look for manna on Saturday (the Sabbath), they found none (*Exodus*16: 22-29).

The evangelist also told the people about the Roman Emperor, Constantine the Great, who thought that it was better for people to rest and go to church on Sundays instead of Saturdays, so in A.D. 321, Constantine passed a law stipulating that in the Catholic Church, Sunday would be the new Sabbath, although nowhere in the Bible was that change ordered or even recommended. He also discussed St. Luke 23: 52-56 and 24: 1, pointing out that although Jesus died on a Friday evening—the day we now commemorate as Good Friday—His disciples did not prepare His body for burial that evening because they wanted to rest and honor the Sabbath Day.

Then someone in the gathering said to the preacher, "I've heard that when Christ died, the law was nailed to the cross with Him and became nul and void, so we don't have to observe the law anymore. Isn't that so?" The evangelist's immediate response was to read the following passage from Jesus's "Sermon on the Mount" in order to prove that statement incorrect:

> Think not that I am come to destroy the law, or the prophets: I am not come to destroy, but to fulfil. For verily I say unto you, Till heaven and earth pass, one jot or one tittle shall in no wise pass from the law, till all be fulfilled. Whosoever therefore shall break one of these least commandments, and shall teach men so, he shall be called the least in the kingdom of heaven: but whosoever shall do and teach them, the same shall be called great in the kingdom of heaven. (*Matthew* 5: 17-19)

Needless to say, my grandparents became Seventh-day Adventists on that day. And so, posthumous recognition and thanks go to my mother, Mary Elizabeth Buntin, for being instrumental in the existence of the New Carmel Church in Salem as well as all other Seventh-day Adventist churches in the island of Montserrat. I have included a Tribute to the New Carmel Seventh-day Adventist Church as my Commentary in this chapter.

Seventh-day Adventist churches have made prolific growth in various parts of the world, often starting as small groups in private homes, until by faith and hard labor, membership and church building funds multiply. This is exactly the way that the Tabernacle Seventh-day Adventist Church grew from its inception. In 1992, when Tabernacle celebrated its fifteenth anniversary, I wrote the following poem as a tribute. I wrote it from a first person confessional point of view for the sake of effect:

Come Let Us Tabernacle Together!

Though I was once a fledgling church,
I am now a giant in North Dade.
Though sometimes my sanctuary seems vacated,
I am not disheartened, for in fifteen years,
My population growth has accelerated.
Though my mortgage is now outstanding,
It will eventually be dissipated.
Though my walls are chipping and my paint is peeling,
I will be renovated.
Within these material walls, for fifteen years,
Infants have been dedicated,
The youth have been educated,
Seniors have been rejuvenated,
Many pastors and elders have pontificated,
The congregation has been stimulated,
And many lives have been reconsecrated.
With the aid of my baptismal font,
Transgressions have been expiated,
And old habits have been eradicated.
Against these walls, from alpha to omega,
Melodic choral strains have reverberated,
And as we congregated,
Our myriad voices enunciated praises to God.
On Sabbaths, we gather as one big family,
And food is masticated.
For fifteen years, last rites have been articulated,
And for the bereaved families,
Benediction has been supplicated.
After Andrew, because of me,
Community loss has been compensated.
In my pews, hundreds of saints have meditated,
And many marriages have been celebrated!
Within these walls,

Constructive plans have been orchestrated,
And conflicts have been mitigated.
Now, and in the future,
Peace, harmony, and bliss will be proliferated.
Come, let us tabernacle together!

Delpha Charles, Ph.D.

The Coconut Grove SDA Church: Keep Striving!

WHERE THE TWO'S AND THREE'S ARE GATHERED IN HIS NAME.......

I would be guilty of untoward remissness if I did not pay tribute to a tiny church—a shining light, a flickering flame—that has remained a fledgling from its nascent stage. After several decades, it is still floundering, still struggling to be airborne. But even in this stage, it is making a difference. Though its members are very few, the impact that these faithful few have made and are making in the Coconut Grove community is admirable. From pastor to officers to the smallest member, their collective energy is palpable and impressive. Though some contribute much more time and effort than others, the fact is manifest that all the members join hearts and hands in a united effort to make a difference in the Grove.

From week to week, the members of this little church are harbingers of cheer to young and old in its environs. In addition to giving Bible studies, they regularly distribute food and clothing to the needy and provide counseling and guidance for groups of youths and seniors. The people of the Grove truly appreciate the service that these church members offer. From its limited resources, this church sets aside the amount required to support this ministry.

Approximately one year ago, someone asked me, "Why are you still affiliated with this little, insignificant church after all these years?" Let me share the answer I provided with my readers:

---These faithful few are special to me.

---I was with them from the early days when they worshiped in the schoolroom.

---It was at this little church (years ago) that I first acquired the courage to play the piano to accompany the congregation on Sabbaths, at the bidding and encouragement of the members, particularly the First Elder. Whether I worship with them four Sabbaths in each year or forty, every time I provide music for church services, I am making a small contribution in my little corner of the Lord's vineyard.

And now to the Grove Church family I say, "Carry on! Keep up the good work!" I know that these energetic workers are desperately seeking, hoping to acquire the funds to build a church. They often worship under a tent, and even in a church without walls, they labor tirelessly. I do believe that one day, the Coconut Grove Seventh-day Adventist Church will have an impressive building and membership. One day, it will be a powerful lighthouse, a beacon for all who are storm-tossed.

The Perrine SDA Church: Another Fledgling Soars

Several decades ago, a courageous, dedicated family of Adventists from New York, having settled in the Perrine vicinity, conceived the idea of a church which , like many other churches, started as a nucleus—a mere kernel—in the homes of this family.

I became affiliated with the Perrine Seventh-day Adventist Church many years ago after the membership had grown considerably, and services were then held in a rented building. Even now, I recall making my small contribution Sabbath after Sabbath, as I played the piano for church services. The fellowship was good at the Perrine Church, and though I no longer worship there, I still feel connected somehow. Actually, I still feel like a "Perrinean." Or, is the word "Perrinite"?

Naturally, I rejoiced with the pastors and members when they brought their construction vision to fruition by dint of hard work. They traveled far by faith and were successful in constructing their own attractive church building. Each time I visit, I experience a vicarious feeling of accomplishment, wishing only that the building were bigger.

To my family and friends at the Perrine Seventh-day Adventist Church, I say "WELL DONE!"

Give Faith a Chance

In discussing Shakespeare's church attendance and my church affiliations, I recognize that millions of people deem "tabernacling" together or church attendance a vain or even naïve exercise, since they insist that there is no proof that God exists. Many espouse the Epicurean-Lucretian philosophy that "the claims of all religions are mythology for there's no evidence for anything beyond this life" (*Anu Bantu 325).* Actually, the Bible is replete with evidence that God exists, but here's the dilemma: the Bible cannot be used to document its own validity. Faith must take over where evidence seems lacking. To all those who accept the Epicurean-Lucretian philosophy, I say give me my so-called "mythology." I must ask them, What if there is, indeed, an after life with a heaven and a hell? Wouldn't it be better to wake up one day after death and discover that presumed reality was mythology? What could be the damage then? But here's a dismal outcome: to be confronted in the after life with stark, God-centered reality previously thought to be "mythology." What then?

Granted, many questions remain unanswered about the inscrutable plan of God—for instance, the existence of evil and the fact that it often triumphs over good. One explanation proffered for this dilemma is that the good is sometimes hidden from the naked human eye. However, some evil is so stark that it is impervious to any semblance of good. Therefore, this explanation seems weak, at best; and yet I am one of those who say, "Give Faith a chance!"

Here are a number of questions I would like to ask atheists, agnostics, existentialists, and all who seek evidence of God's existence:

> Do all the wonders and the vastness of the cosmos count for naught?

Of the evolutionists I ask, Who created the three states of matter—solid, liquid, and gas—the material that is said to have exploded? Where did this original material that allegedly caused the so-called big bang come from?

And what about plasma which is the most common form of matter in the universe—manifested in the sun and stars? Where did plasma (often considered the fourth state of matter) come from? Who created it?

Let's not forget protoplasm—a name that Hugo von Mohl coined in 1846 for the substance that composes (wholly or in part) all living cells, tissues, or organisms of any kind. Who created protoplasm-- organic : proteins, carbohydrates, lipids, nucleic acids, enzymes and inorganic: water, mineral salts, and gases (e.g. oxygen and carbon dioxide)?

Must we believe that we are simple balls of protoplasm walking about by chance or accident, not design?

Is the complex, intricate miracle of the human body, with its patterned, ordered trillions of cells, to be dismissed so lightly?

Let's take a moment to consider this fact: Every cell in the human body has DNA (deoxyribonucleic acid) at its core in the forty-six chromosomes. DNA is 99.9% the same in all humans. It is that crucial .1% which is different in all humans that guards our individualism, our uniqueness. It is this all-important .1% that facilitates the work of forensic scientists and enable them to identify criminals, beyond doubt. Isn't that fascinating? My question is, Who planned that difference? What Master Hand, what Master Mind prevented us from being simply cellular carbon copies of one another? The only obvious answer is God.

Of course, nonbelievers may dismiss all that I have written thus far and will consider fictitious what is written in the gospels (example: St. John 20 and 21)—that the resurrected Christ appeared several times to His disciples before His ascension into heaven. However, though Biblical statements may be discounted, **historical facts cannot be denied. The evidence that nonbelievers seek is documented in the annals of history:** To all Epicurean-Lucretian thinkers, let me hasten to say that Jesus Christ of Nazareth was no "myth." Volumes of historical documents verify the fact that He walked this earth over two thousand years ago. **So what is the evidence that Christ is God and, therefore, God does exist? An empty tomb is the evidence. Ironically, Roman history provides the evidence we seek.** Let me explain.

The Romans were proud, imperious, indomitable people. Their leaders considered themselves on par with their many gods, never expecting to be vanquished in any contest. Therefore, would they have placed minimum security at the tomb of a man who (they thought) not only dared to challenge Caesar but, what's worse, also threatened to rise again after three days and perhaps come after them to seek retribution? Impossible! Not only would they have feared the retaliation that such a return to life would have brought, but such a reappearance would also have proved the crucified prisoner to be immortal, while they remained mere mortals. They would not, could not have allowed that! So, would they have stationed just a few soldiers at the entrance to that sepulcher? No! Not the mighty, vengeful Romans who are etched in the history books I have read. Not the unconquerable Romans who traveled thousands of miles and relentlessly laid siege for months and months, leveling fortresses and conquering kingdom after kingdom, across the ancient world, just to prove a point.

No, the Romans would have placed stone upon stone, granite upon granite, and assign centurions with their legions the responsibility to keep that special tomb secure. And, in the Roman way of thinking, just in case the disciples of the crucified prisoner had any tricks up their sleeves like hiding the body and falsely claiming resurrection, the Romans quite possibly kept all the disciples in their purview, under strict surveillance.

And that's not all. After death, even if only partial body parts could have been found, wouldn't the Romans have victoriously held them up to the world to say, "Aha, we told you he was a fake! King in Jerusalem, Ha! Ha! Caesar is king/emperor, not he!" Then they may have hastened to build the biggest tombstone—one that might have claimed a place as the eighth Wonder of the ancient world—to mark the spot where they acquired such an important victory. They might have placed an inscription like this one on that tomb: "Here Lies an Upstart from Nazareth Who Dared to Challenge Caesar!" And even if they decided to do the opposite and bury Him like a common criminal in an unmarked spot somewhere in the desert, you can bet that Roman history would have been replete with references to the vanquished Christ, and the Romans would have been proud to proclaim that His bones still lie in the desert. But not a single such reference exists. None of these events occurred.

In fact, a totally different outcome flashes before our eyes. The Roman braggadocio was brought to a resounding, humbling silence when those soldiers encountered <u>the gaping, empty tomb</u>. The laughter died; the scoffing ended.

The Romans must have asked themselves a thousand questions to which they, themselves, would have supplied the answers: Did He come to do what He said He would do, and now has He returned to His Father? Is He really the Son of God? Is He really going to come again as the Messianic King? Were we wrong to consider Him a mere mortal? **Obviously, they answered "yes" to all of these questions because one by one, these powerful Roman emperors and other leaders—erstwhile pagans all—became Christians and believers in God—Jehovah—and Jesus Christ, His Son.**

Constantine the Great who imposed Sunday worship was quite possibly the best known Christian convert among the Roman emperors. But history has recorded the most famous, the most fascinating and dramatic Christian conversion ever: that of Saul of Tarsus. After he encountered Christ on the road to Damascus, he changed from persecutor to preacher and became the greatest Christian missionary, later known as St. Paul.

Though much of Shakespeare's church affiliation remains unknown, the following passages from his works demonstrate that religion played a role, even a minor one, in his life. His characters, rich and poor—great and small—pray continually for God's help to overcome difficulties. The following quote is King Henry V's prayer just before he engages the French army in the famous Battle of Agincourt (1415). We can assume that Shakespeare believed not only in God but also in prayer.

O God of Battles, Steel My Soldiers' Hearts!

O God of battles, steel my soldiers'
Hearts!
Possess them not with fear, take from them now
The sense of reckoning if the oppose`d numbers
Pluck their hearts from them. Not today, O Lord,
Oh, not today, think not upon the fault
My father made in compassing the crown!***
I Richard's body have interre`d new,

And on it have bestowed more contrite tears
Than from it issued force'd drops of blood.
Five hundred poor I have in yearly pay,
Who twice a day their withered hands hold up
Toward Heaven, to pardon blood, and I have built
Two chantries where the sad and solemn priests
Sing still for Richard's soul. More will I do,
Though all that I can do is nothing worth,
Since that my penitence comes after all,
Imploring pardon.
(*Henry V* 4. 1. 307-322)

***NOTE:** King Henry IV of England (Henry V's father) occupied the throne that rightfully belonged to Richard II. Several years later, this deposition triggered the Wars of the Roses—the long contest for the throne of England (1455-84) between the houses of Lancaster (badge—red rose) and York (badge—white rose).

PARAPHRASE

O God who controls warfare, imbue courage in the hearts of my soldiers! Don't let them be fearful. Take away the thought of defeat if they are overwhelmed when they see the tremendous size of the opposing army. Don't choose today, Lord, to punish me for the fact that my father unlawfully occupied the throne! I have given Richard's body fresh burial rites, and I have shed more repentant tears over his body than the drops of blood that fell from his punctured body. I have paid five hundred peasants yearly, and they have stretched forth their shriveled hands twice daily towards heaven asking for pardon for the shedding of Richard's blood. And I have built two chapels where the sorrowful and downcast priests sing continuously for Richard's soul. I will do more, even though all I can do means nothing since my contrition is, above all, the greatest indication of my sincere prayer for forgiveness.

And My Ending Is Despair

And my ending is despair
Unless I be relieved by prayer***
Which pierces so that it assaults
Mercy itself, and frees all faults.
(*Tempest*, Epilogue 15-18)

***NOTE: Shakespeare makes reference to prayer repeatedly in many of his plays. Once more, as he speaks through his characters, we see that quite possibly Shakespeare believed that prayer can indeed make a difference for the better in human existence.

PARAPHRASE

My life will end in despondency if my spirit is not lifted and buoyed up by prayer so powerful that it virtually confronts Mercy (personified) and compels him to forgive all of my demerits.

The World Is Still Deceived with Ornament

The world is still deceived with ornament.
In law, what plea so tainted and corrupt
But, being seasoned with a gracious voice,
Obscures the show of evil? In religion,
What damne`d error but some sober brow
Will bless it, and approve it with a text,
Hiding the grossness with fair ornament?
(*The Merchant of Venice* 3. 2. 74-80)

***NOTE:** Shakespeare may have believed in prayer, but through this character (Bassanio), he has some disparaging words for the church, alleging that church personnel are often as deceptive and corrupt as members of the legal profession who seek to disguise evil and present it as good and acceptable. Similarly, church personnel often bless or cover up sinful acts and make them tolerable, he claims.

PARAPHRASE

The world is always deluded by outward appearances. In the legal profession, what case, no matter how polluted or debased, cannot be sanitized by a smooth-talking lawyer, thus hiding the underlying evil? In religion, what transgression, no matter how blatant or vile, will not be deemed acceptable after some religious authority endorses it and even presents a Biblical text that allegedly justifies it and white washes it?

COMMENTARY: A Tribute to New Carmel My First Church

The Introduction to this chapter highlights the circumstances surrounding the emergence of the New Carmel Seventh-day Adventist Church in Montserrat. My life began at my infant baptism in this church which was the first institution to exert a guiding influence on me. Here is where I was "offered up," as the vernacular puts it. Many Montserratian Adventists returned to Salem in 1991 from the various diasporas around the world—England, America, Canada, as well as other Caribbean islands—to celebrate New Carmel's Seventy-fifth Anniversary. I also went "home" to New Carmel and wrote the following piece to commemorate Seventy-Five Years of Adventism in the island of Montserrat. I deemed it fitting to include this tribute to New Carmel as my Commentary in this chapter.

> I celebrate myself, and sing myself,
> And what I assume you shall assume,
> For every atom belonging to me as good belongs to you.
> ....
> My tongue, every atom of my blood, form'd from this soil, this air,
> Born here of parents born here from parents the same,
> and their parents the same,
> ....
> Prodigal, you have given me love—therefore I to you give love!

The above words were written by Walt Whitman (1819-92) in his famous work entitled *Leaves of Grass.* In Whitmanesque fashion, I celebrate each blade of grass that grows from the soil that cushions you, New Carmel. You deserve clarion recognition and unequivocal praise. Each diaspora of New Carmelites in North America, Canada, England, and in various other parts of the world is a symbol of your nurturing—a sprout from your granite roots. We, as fledgling New Carmelites, went into the world to disseminate the discipline and the values we cultivated in your pews. You were not founded on the plains of Mesopotamia to monitor the incipient stages of civilization; nor were you cradled among the Egyptian pyramids. You do not rival Westminster Abbey; nor do you presume to the material grandeur of the Vatican. You do not share the worldly acclaim of the Notre Dame. Yet by no means is your spot on planet earth a "mute inglorious" one. As a child and adolescent, I was not aware of the enduring foundation you were laying and the indelible mark you were registering on my life.

As I interacted with my mother, father, sisters, and brother in a carefree childhood, you were an ever-present, personified extension of my family, endorsing or reechoing the values my parents instilled in us. Each day, my siblings and I were taught to love one another. Each Sabbath, my community "siblings" heard that lesson reiterated in hymns such as "Love One Another Thus Saith the Saviour." Granted, as in most mother-daughter relationships, I went through my period of protest. Oh! There were times in my childhood when I was less than happy with you. Sometimes I felt like rebelling when I had to fast at your behest or when my father and mother stopped me in my tracks for family worship just before sunset each Friday afternoon, regardless of how urgently I wished to finish what I was doing. However, as my mother sang her favorites "The Sun Rolls down the Distant West" and "Safely Through Another Week" (on Friday evenings) as well as "Far from All Care" (on Sabbath mornings), I quickly settled down. As a child, I also felt inclined to protest each "Old Year's Eve" when I had to sit in your pews instead of being allowed to watch the colorful masquerades for the last lap. But I learned discipline early.

As if by osmosis, in your pews, I absorbed the sturdy principles that govern my life to this very moment. I was a fun-loving child and a light-hearted teenager who took neither my studies nor the world seriously. However, gradually, imperceptibly, you implanted in me worthwhile values that saw me through my girlhood and are a vital part of my adulthood. As I watched and listened to my aunt at the organ Sabbath after Sabbath, I developed an insatiable appetite for music. My abiding ambition was to emulate her when I grew up. Today, each Sabbath at two churches in America, I play (at the piano) the identical hymns she played decades ago. Those old favorite hymns I first lisped in your

8. WORK ETHIC

INTRODUCTION

The pronouncement was made in Eden: "In the sweat of thy face shalt thou eat bread. . . ." *(Genesis 3:19)*. Work is a condition of life that mankind inherited. Some among us embrace it willingly; others accept it as a necessary evil. Still others seek to avoid it at all cost. There are those who go to their jobs readily, even eagerly, each day. Others (the majority) go kicking and screaming everyday, impatiently awaiting the age of retirement.

Shakespeare as well as King Solomon wisely advised us to draw valuable lessons regarding our work ethic from the stringently organized colonies of two of nature's tiniest creatures: the ants and the bees. What perpetual toil! What industry! How fascinating to watch them work! What organization; what corporation; what a phenomenon! Solomon admonishes, "Go to the ant, thou sluggard; consider her ways, and be wise" (*Proverbs* 6:6).

Regardless of our attitude towards work, whether we see it as a blessing or a curse, whether we work outside the home or in it or both, whether we work mentally or physically or both, whether we are wealthy or penniless, we work because we are human. That's why when we lose a job, we look for another. Society frowns at those who sit around and refuse to work. Regardless of the form it takes, working is an endemic part of our humanity. St. Paul declares, ". . .If any would not work, neither should he eat" (2*Thessalonians* 3: 10). Since God commissioned us to work, we can conclude that sitting around not working (especially when dependent children are involved) is sinful. In old age, there will be plenty of time for sitting.

Like Solomon, St. Paul, and Shakespeare, Sigmund Freud deems work the act that makes us most poignantly human. He asserts: "No other technique for the conduct of life attaches the individual so firmly to reality as laying emphasis on work; for his work at least gives him a secure place in a portion of reality, in the human community."

Weary with Toil

Weary with toil, I haste me to my bed,
The dear repose for limbs with travel tired.
But then begins a journey in my head,
To work my mind, when body's work's expired.
For then my thoughts, from far where I abide,
Intend a zealous pilgrimage to thee,

pews (and later sang lustily) have formed a substantial part of my psyche. For example, the work ethic was riveted in me as I sang "Working, O Christ, with Thee." I learned early that nothing worthwhile comes but by dint of toil. "Work for the Night Is Coming When Man Works No More" meant very little to a five year old who sang along with the patriarchs and matriarchs in your pews. But later, I was able to recognize the "carpe diem" philosophy—the necessity to "make hay while the sun shines." In "Let Every Lamp Be Burning Bright" I looked past symbolism to visualize the very real dilemma of the five foolish virgins, and I grasped the need for planning and watchfulness in my endeavors.

    These and other worthwhile principles I was able to pass on to my students at Oakwood College, Howard University, Miami-Dade College, the University of Miami, Florida International University, and all other institutions where I have served as an instructor or professor. Living for the major part of my life in pluralistic, materialistic North America, I have recalled from time to time the hymn "Lord I Care Not for Riches, Neither Silver Nor Gold," and I have seen the significance of the tenet, "The love of money is the root of all evil." I was often buoyed up when I recalled the strains of "Heir of the Kingdom" and "My Father Is Rich in Houses and Land." Only as an adult I fully realized the significance of being heir to celestial rather than terrestrial wealth.

    At four, five, six, and seven years old, I had visions (even nightmares) of some poor soul thrashing around in Isles Bay, sinking fast, waiting for someone to "throw out the life line" to him. Our youthful minds play strange tricks on us; therefore, for some unknown reason, I envisioned a positive aftermath to this almost tragic scene. Nestled between my mother and my older sisters, I actually rejoiced and secretly thanked someone by the name of "Love" who took pity and "lifted" the almost lifeless body from those towering waves. From those early years in your pews, I learned through those lyrics that I am indeed my brother's keeper and that I should do all I can to minister to my earthly siblings regardless of color, creed, or ethnicity. Of course, after I matured, I rejoiced even more when I was able to conceptualize the true theme of "Love Lifted Me"—the wonderful redemptive act and its consequences.

    Freud and other psychologists tell us that our childhood, to a large extent, determines who we are in adulthood. The feelings of security or, conversely, insecurity developed in childhood often linger and affect us later. Wordsworth assents in his assertion that "The child is father of the man." As I sat in your pews, like many other four, five, and six year olds, I had the vision of Good Mrs. Murphy following me around "all the days of my life," contributing to my sense of security and belonging. There was no likelihood of my being a maladjusted child. In a very real sense, therefore, I owe much of what I am today to you, my Alma Mater. This daughter says, "THANK YOU!"

And keep my drooping eyelids open wide,
Looking on darkness which the blind do see.
Save that my soul's imaginary sight
Presents thy shadow to my sightless view,
Which, like a jewel hung in ghastly night,
Makes black night beauteous and her old face new.
    Lo, thus by day my limbs, by night my mind,
    For thee and for myself no quiet find.
    (*Sonnet* 27)

PARAPHRASE

Tired after working, I hurry to bed to give my weary bones sweet rest. But at that point, my mind takes up the activity my body has laid down because from a distance, my thoughts begin to travel towards you, keeping my heavy eyelids wide open. In my imagination, I see your image, like a jewel, with renewed facial beauty shining in the darkness. Therefore, work is a constant for me: my body works during the day, and my mind works at nights.

Therefore Doth Heaven Divide the State of Man

    Therefore doth Heaven divide
The state of man in divers functions,
Setting endeavor in continual motion.
To which is fixed, as an aim or butt,
Obedience. For so work the honeybees,
Creatures that by a rule in nature teach
The act of order to a peopled kingdom.
They have a King and officers of sorts,
Where some, like magistrates, correct at home,
Others, like merchants, venture trade abroad,
Others, like soldiers, armed in their stings,
Make boot upon the summer's velvet buds,

Which pillage they with merry march bring home
To the tent royal of their Emperor.
Who, busied in his majesty, surveys
The singing masons building roofs of gold,
The civil citizens kneading up the honey,
The poor mechanic porters crowding in
Their heavy burdens at his narrow gate,
The sad-eyed Justice, with his surly hum,
Delivering o'er to executor's pale
The lazy yawning drone.
(*Henry V* 1. 2. 183-213)

*****NOTE:** In this passage, Shakespeare uses a popular conceit: a parallel between a beehive and a kingdom. And what a true similarity does indeed exist. Whether a kingdom, a nation, a town, or even a village, the survival of any community depends on order, organization, rules, hard work, and united effort. Mother Nature effectively drives home the importance of collective labor. Notice the message here: those who do not work or help to build—the drones—are handed over to the authorities to be punished to the fullest extent of the law.

PARAPHRASE

Therefore, heaven controls the welfare of mankind by making people productive in a variety of roles, setting the stage for ever-increasing achievement. The underlying impulse for man's strivings is his inherent, perhaps unwitting, obedience to the heaven-ordained edict stipulating the need to work. This work imperative is seen in the lifestyle (activities) of the honeybees. By a natural law, these insects teach order, discipline, and cooperation to the inhabitants of kingdoms or large communities. In a hive, there is a king as well as officers of different ranks. Some, like magistrates (judges), keep order in the colony. Others, like merchants, traffic in other communities. Others, like soldiers, carry their weapons in their stings, as they plunder the lush blossoms of summer and bring home their booty, in a triumphant march, to the royal domain of their Emperor who, in his majestic role, is busy surveying the masons who are singing as they build golden roofs. The courteous citizens are piling up the honey, and the hardworking members of the laboring class strenuously carry their heavy cargo to the narrow gate of the king. The sober Judge buzzes imperiously as he passes judgment on the slothful drone and hands him over to the executioners.

There Is No Ancient Gentlemen

There is no ancient
gentlemen but gardeners, ditchers, and gravemakers.
They hold up Adam's profession.***
(*Hamlet* 5. 1. 33-35)

***NOTE: Once more, Shakespeare refers to the edict in Eden when God orders Adam (the first human) to work in order to survive. Mankind's work imperative started here.

PARAPHRASE

There is no group of elderly men that does not contain gardeners, ditch diggers, or grave diggers. Since this was the type of work done by Adam (God gave Adam and Eve the responsibility to "dress" or tend the Garden of Eden), he was a gardener even before the Fall. Regardless of the type of work, human beings are expected to "hold up" or continue what Adam started: they should work for a living as long as they can do so.

What a Piece of Work Is Man!

What a piece of work is man! How noble in reason! How infinite in faculty! In form and moving how express and admirable! In action how like an angel! In apprehension how like a god! The beauty of the world! The paragon of animals! And yet, to me, what is this quintessence of dust?
(*Hamlet 2. 2.315-320*)

*****NOTE:** Here, Shakespeare seems to be reminding us that even God (Jehovah) Himself worked to create man during the week of Creation (See *Genesis* 2:7). He created man on day number six and then created and rested the Sabbath.

PARAPHRASE

What magnificent handiwork is mankind! How ample (lofty) is his rational ability! How vast is the power of his mind! In structure and movement how exact and impressive! In behavior how angelic! How godlike in his acquisition of knowledge! Mankind is the most beautiful being on earth! The most excellent among all other animals! And yet, what is mankind but simply the better part of dust?

COMMENTARY: The Catch of the Day in Salem

Everyone in the Salem Community knew that at the sound of the conch shell, it was time to hurry to the central meeting place in front of Mr. Walker's grocery store to purchase fish for the evening meal. The fishermen exposed their catch of the day with pride while they dickered with the housewives who were eager for a bargain. And all the while, from the western boundary of the island, the mighty ocean seemed to look on with a measure of satisfaction at having yielded up an adequate day's supply of protein for Salem's households.

In the opposite direction, at the extreme eastern end of the island, the lofty mountain loomed large in majestic silence as if patiently waiting its turn, stolid, tranquil, yet eager to contribute its supply of protein as the sea had done so graciously earlier. Both—at opposite ends of the island of Montserrat—seemed to compete in their effort to substantiate the élan vital—the energy—of the bustling crowds that populated the Salem Community.

Every evening, the gracious mountain beckoned a lonely, familiar figure that approached it with unwavering steps. Nothing deterred him. Not old age. Not decrepitude. Not steep, rocky, winding footpaths. Not the many miles he had to climb to reach the imposing mountain. Like Wordsworth's Leech-gatherer, he ambled forward with "resolution and independence," determined to gain "an honest maintenance."

With a crocus sack slung over his shoulder, and with an air of expectancy, Leroy Bain wended his way towards the mountain, confident that his night's labor would pay off in good dividends the following day. Each evening, the villagers watched him go, knowing that he would spend the night with the frogs that inhabit the mountain. Throughout the night, he would catch as many as he could and place them in his crocus bag. Each morning, at sunrise, the villagers would see Leroy Bain returning with a bulging crocus bag slung over his shoulder. It was common knowledge that his destination was the fashionable bayside hotel resort where many American and Canadian tourists waited impatiently to order what they deemed the delectable entrée—mountain chicken.

I recall that each time I stayed at the hotel on my vacations in Montserrat, on each menu, quite often mountain chicken would be featured as the "Special of the Day." I usually smiled while I desperately looked for something else, anything else, on the menu. Of course, those who prepared the meals were oblivious of the fact that my irrational fear of frogs was only one among a number of reasons that would compel me to choose an alternate entrée.

Those of us who "Love Lucy" may recall the hilarious episode in Paris when Lucy has difficulty eating escargot (snails). Well, even if I had borrowed Lucy's escargot clamps and placed them on my nose, as she had done, I would still have found it impossible to eat the mountain chicken. But the point I seek to emphasize is the work ethic—the hard work, the determination and independence, the admirable thrift—of this unforgettable old man, Leroy Bain.

9. RAPE

INTRODUCTION

She half ran, half walked, half limped across the yard of the neighborhood school, still incredulous as she reflected on what had just transpired in one of the classrooms. Mr. Lucas, principal of one of the leading schools in St. John's, Antigua, had made an appointment with her to tutor her in math for an hour or two after school as she prepared for the London O Level Exam. Esther was pleased and grateful that this respected headmaster was kind enough to offer to help her. Therefore, at the end of the day, after she had dismissed her students at another school in St. John's, she walked across town to meet Mr. Lucus in his office at school, as he had instructed her to do.

Shortly after she entered the room and sat in the first available chair, she noticed that there were no books on Mr. Lucas's desk. He suggested that he and Esther could read from the same book, and he sat beside her. Suddenly, she felt two strong arms embrace her. She jumped up, startled and afraid. In one or two swift movements, Mr. Lucas locked the door and wrestled her to the floor. Esther screamed for help from a janitor perhaps, from anyone, but she screamed in vain. No one was around to help her. As she and Mr. Lucas thrashed around on the floor, her hand brushed against the leg of a chair. Grasping the chair, she hurled it at him in desperation. She then struggled to her feet, raced across the room, and jumped out of the nearest window. Panting, sweating, and disheveled, she arrived home. Her relatives were surprised and outraged to hear that Mr. Lucas, whom everyone considered a gentleman, had attempted to rape her.

Rape is more prevalent than can be imagined. From ancient to modern days, from Biblical days to post-Biblical times, it has reared its ugly head. It is a cross-cultural scourge. It is a scurrilous, inhuman act of violence that often destroys its victims emotionally and tears families apart. But the most repulsive, the most intolerable, the most vile form of rape is pedophilic molestation. Almost not a day goes by that we do not hear of yet another childhood molestation in America among rich and poor alike, among famous and nonfamous, across ethnic lines. Rapists or molestors of children are often baby sitters, neighbors, teachers, coaches, family members, friends of family, even church members and officers.

Like America as well as other countries in all parts of the earth, the Caribbean islands have had their share of episodes involving rape. A number of teenagers, adolescents, and even pre-adolescent girls in Montserrat and Antigua were raped, molested, touched, or seduced by older cousins, step fathers, uncles, neighbors, and family friends. Several years ago, in Antigua, the botonical park located on the eastern side of St. John's was a place where one or two notorious rapists lurked waiting for their unsuspecting prey. Recently, in the headline news in America, we have heard of even senior citizens being overpowered and raped.

Rape was no stranger to Shakespeare's world. It is one of his hot topics, featured most extensively in two of his works: *The Tragedy of Titus Andronicus* and the poem *The Rape of Lucrece*. In the Shakespearean episodes, rape is so extreme a violation and devastation that it usually becomes a precursor of death to the victim. It is as if in each incident, death is necessary after the act to blot out the shame and enable the victim to achieve some measure of purging or cleansing. Therefore, the virginal Lavinia is killed by her father after she is raped (*Titus Andronicus*), and the noble lady Lucrece kills herself after she is violated (*The Rape of Lucrece*). Here is a brief synopsis of these two works:

The Tragedy of Titus Andronicus

The details of this tragedy are gruesome indeed. The action involves unspeakable, wanton bloodshed—senseless, gratuitous destruction and mutilation—yet, unfortunately, some modern crime scenes are comparable. Titus Andronicus, a Roman general, returns home after ten years of warfare. He has taken captive Tamora, Queen of the Goths, and her three sons. Most of his sons have been killed in the war, so he sacrifices Tamora's eldest son to appease their deaths. In revenge, Tamora schemes and has two of Titus' sons beheaded. She also urges her sons Chiron and Demetrius to rape Titus' daughter Lavinia, after which they cut off her hands and cut out her tongue to prevent her from disclosing the violation she has suffered. Titus later kills Chiron and Demetrius, makes a pie with their bodies, and feeds this pie to their unsuspecting mother. He later kills her as well as his own daughter and has Tamora's body thrown to the dogs (remember Jezebel?).

The Rape of Lucrece

The story of the fate of Lucrece was part of Roman legend and was told by Livy and Ovid. Few stories were more popular in Elizabethan England. Here's a very brief synopsis:

Sextus Tarquinius, a Roman ruler, travels abroad surrounded by his courtiers. He listens as these noblemen extol the virtues of their wives. The one who peaks his interest is Lucrece, Collatinus' wife. One night, while her husband is away, Tarquinius travels to her home, sneaks into her bedroom, overpowers her, stifles her desperate protests, and ravishes her. She later kills herself.

Lavinia, Wert Thou Thus Surprised

Lavinia, wert thou thus surprised, sweet girl,
Ravished and wronged, as Philomela was,
Forced in the ruthless, vast, and gloomy woods?
See, see!
Aye, such a place there is, where we did hunt—
. . . .
By nature made for murders and for rapes.
(*The Tragedy of Titus Andronicus* 4. 1. 51-58)

PARAPHRASE

Lavinia, were you taken by surprise like this, dear girl? Were you raped and violated like Philomela,*** overpowered in the dismal, sprawling, dark and desolate woods? Look! Look! Yes, there's a place that fits that description—a place where we hunted—a place designed by nature to facilitate murders and rapes.

***NOTE:** In Greek mythology, Philomel was a young girl who was raped and also had her tongue cut out. She was changed into a nightingale by the Gods.

But She Hath Lost a Dearer Thing than Life

But she hath lost a dearer thing than life,
And he hath won what he would lose again.
This forced league doth force a further strife;
This momentary joy breeds months of pain;
This hot desire converts to cold disdain.
Pure Chastity is rifled of her store,
And Lust, the thief, far poorer than before.
(*The Rape of Lucrece 687-93*)

PARAPHRASE

But she (the victim) has lost something more precious than life. And he (the rapist) has won something he cannot keep (retain). This forced union leads to future turbulence. This temporary pleasure causes months of suffering. This fiery appetite quickly changes to scorn. Innocence—virtue—is robbed or depleted, and the thief, Lust, has gained nothing, being far poorer than he was before.

As the Poor Frighted Deer

As the poor frighted deer, that stands at gaze,
Wildly determining which way to fly,

Or one encompassed with a winding maze,
That cannot tread the way out readily,
So with herself is she in mutiny,
To live or die, which of the twain were better,
When life is shamed and death reproach's debtor.
(*The Rape of Lucrece 1149-55*)

PARAPHRASE

Like a poor frightened deer that stands confused and frenzied, unsure of a means of escape, or like someone caught in a complex maze without an easy exit, she (Lucrece) is torn with internal conflict, unable to decide whether it is better to live or die when a shamed life should end in suicide.

COMMENTARY: An Incident I'll Never Forget

Whenever I read *The Rape of Lucrece*, I usually recall an incident in my life. Travel back with me mentally several decades. Let us use the present tense to relive the incident. I am a freshman student at Howard University in Washington, D.C. I am living off campus in a private home, to which I was referred by the University, since there is no room in the dorms. My landlady (Mrs. Bolton) is a kind elderly woman, and she and I occupy the modest house which has three small bedrooms upstairs, a living room, dining room, and kitchen on the first floor, and a basement accessed from the kitchen.

Shortly after I arrive at the home, Mrs. Bolton introduces me to the other occupants of her home: Theresa, another student, has the third bedroom upstairs, and Peter Smith—a young man who works in the city—is a tenant occupying the basement.

Mrs. Bolton and Theresa are the only people with whom I interact on a daily basis. We often chat and laugh and eat together in the kitchen. Mr. Smith is very rarely seen. He never enters any room in the house except his basement apartment which is complete with kitchen, bathroom, and all basic facilities. He uses only the passage that leads from the front door strictly to exit and enter the basement. Each day, when he arrives home from work, he goes straight to the basement and does not emerge until the following day's exit through the front door. On the rare occasion that I might happen to be near the front door on his way in or out, he would say a cordial, respectful good morning or good afternoon and keep going.

After approximately five months, Theresa graduates and moves out. Mrs. Bolton and I are consequently the sole occupants of the first and second floors of the house. One evening, Mrs. Bolton decides to visit and overnight at her daughter's home in the northwestern part of the city. Before leaving, she calls to Mr. Smith, informing him that she would be away for the night. I hear her saying to him, "Keep your ear out. Make sure all is well until I return in the morning."

It is a typical night of the week. As usual, all lights are out on the first floor around ten o'clock. I have several assignments to be completed for my classes the following day. Therefore, I realize that I would have to spend most of the night studying. It is customary for me to go upstairs to my bedroom, put on my night dress, and then prop myself up in bed to read, write, and prepare class work for the next day. Around midnight, I am engrossed in my reading when suddenly I hear someone walking downstairs. The wooden, uncarpeted floor squeaks more loudly and more threateningly than usual. My heart starts pounding violently. Who or what can be walking downstairs at midnight? Is it human? Non human? Is it a burglar?

I hear the footsteps shuffling, pacing, moving slowly from the kitchen to the front door and then back to the kitchen after a brief pause. Over and over, he/it moves from front door to kitchen; from kitchen to front door. After a while, I pluck up the courage to open my bedroom door and look downstairs. Impenetrable darkness greets my eyes, and the pacing continues from the kitchen to the front door. Fear overwhelms me. I recall with paralyzing dismay that my bedroom and the other two bedrooms upstairs have no locks on the doors.

At this moment, just as I am about to collapse from fright, I remember that Mr. Smith occupies the basement of the house. Therefore, I half convince myself that I am not alone. But wait, what if he is the one pacing eerily downstairs in the dark? Even as I ponder the situation, I hear myself calling,
"Mr. Smith! Is that you?"
I am surprised to hear him reply, "Yes."
"You scared me. Is everything all right?" I ask.
"Yes," he replies.
Though I am puzzled at his strange behavior, I go back to my studies somewhat relieved. At least, a burglar did not invade the house.

All is quiet inside and outside the house for approximately ten minutes. As coincidence would have it, I am reading one of Edgar Allan Poe's grotesque narratives for class discussion the following day. Suddenly, I hear the footsteps again—heavy, restless, agitated, calculated steps: from the kitchen to the front door! pause! from the front door to the kitchen! pause! from the kitchen to the front door! pause! from the front door to the—to the—to the—Oh Mercy! to the bottom of the staircase. I hold my breath. Surely, my imagination must be playing tricks on me. But no! Unmistakably, the stillness in the house is shattered by one heavy, squeaky, reverberating footstep after another coming slowly, deliberately up the stairs towards my bedroom.

I am paralyzed with fear. Who or what is approaching me? Is it Mr. Smith? If so, what does he want? Neither he nor any other male has ever been up those stairs. My mind is racing. I glance around desperately for a weapon. There is none. I am thinking fast. Should I jump out the upstairs window and die quickly? Should I speak? Should I scream? But fear has rendered me immobile, speechless, and "screamless." So there I am sitting up in bed, terrified, petrified, braced for whatever I must endure when the footsteps stop at my bedroom door. Naturally, I am praying incessantly, asking God to deliver me. Just before the last footstep lands at my door, the words of *Psalms* 91 rush to my mind:

> ... Thou shalt not be afraid for the terror by night; nor for the arrow that flieth by day; nor for the pestilence that **walketh in darkness**; .... There shall no evil befall thee, neither shall any plague come nigh thy dwelling. For he shall give his angels charge over thee, to keep thee in all thy ways. ... He shall call upon me, and I will answer him: I will be with him in trouble; I will deliver him, and honour him. With long life will I satisfy him, and shew him my salvation.

At that moment, I look up to see Mr. Smith's muscular body framed in the entrance of my bedroom. He looks at me with leering, lustful, bloodshot eyes. There is a strange, contorted look on his face.

"What are you doing?" he asks me.

"I am studying! Why are you up here! What do you want? How dare you come up here! How dare you. . . ." I continue to shout at him.

Without another look, without another word, he turns around and walks back down the stairs.

I have had some close calls in my life. My God has snatched me from the jaws of death on several occasions as I traveled on the highways of America. But that night in Washington, D.C. was one crucial instant when God tangibly put in His appearance and delivered me from rape and possibly death.

10. INCEST

INTRODUCTION

The thought of a father molesting his own daughter is abhorrent and repugnant beyond expression. Though it is such a heinous act, this abomination occurs more frequently than we care to admit. Every now and then, some famous woman comes forward to confess that she has had incestuous relations with her father, starting from childhood. Incest in one form or other occurred even in Biblical times. For example, incest destroyed King David's household. His son Amnon violated his own sister, Tamar, and Absalom (another son) avenged Tamar's rape by killing Amnon (II *Samuel* 13). In some ancient cultures, marriage between sister and brother was permitted, but in most cultures, incest is emphatically taboo. Through his characters, Shakespeare vigorously condemns incest.

Antiochus from Incest Lived Not Free

Antiochus from incest lived not free;
For which, the most high gods not minding longer
To withhold the vengeance that they had in store,
Due to his heinous capital offence,
Even in the height and pride of all his glory,
When he was seated in a chariot
Of an inestimable value, and his daughter with him,
A fire from Heaven came, and shrivelled up
Their bodies, even to loathing; for they so stunk,
That all those eyes adored them, ere their fall,
Scorn now their hand should give them burial.
(*Pericles* 2. 4. 3-12)

PARAPHRASE

Antiochus did not live without indulging in incest. The powerful gods did not wish to hold back punishment for this abominable and deadly sin any longer. At the peak of his glory and majestic splendor, while he and his daughter sat in a priceless chariot, fire descended from heaven and consumed their bodies to such an extent that they were repulsive to behold, and the odor from their bodies was so offensive that all those who worshiped them with their eyes before they died are now reluctant to soil their hands to bury them.

Frailty, Thy Name Is Woman

> --Frailty, thy name is woman!— ***
> A little month, or ere those shoes were old
> With which she followed my poor father's body,
> Like Niobe*** all tears.—Why she, even she—
> Oh, God! A beast that wants discourse of reason
> Would have mourned longer—married with my uncle,
> My father's brother, but no more like my father
> Than I to Hercules. Within a month,
> Ere yet the salt of most unrighteous tears
> Had left the flushing in her galled eyes,
> She married. Oh, most wicked speed, to post
> With such dexterity to incestuous sheets!
> (*Hamlet* 1. 2. 146-157)

***NOTE: Though sometimes regarded an anti-feminist Shakespearean remark, when seen simply from Hamlet's perspective, these words are more readily construed as a bitter protest—an expression of the searing anger he holds for his mother who marries her brother-in-law (Hamlet's uncle) almost immediately after Hamlet's father is murdered. He hates his uncle whom his father's ghost reveals to be the murderer.

***NOTE: In Greek mythology, Niobe was full of pride and bragged excessively about her children, and so the goddess Artemis killed all her children. Thereafter, Niobe cried so much that she was changed into a rock that forever dripped water.

PARAPHRASE

A woman's name is synonymous with weakness (i. e. All women are weak). Imagine, after only one short month, before there is any wear or tear on the shoes she wore to my poor father's funeral, all the while weeping incessantly like Niobe—Dear God! Even a beast that lacks the ability to reason would have mourned longer. She is married to my uncle, my father's brother, but he is no more like my father than I am like Hercules. In one month, before the salt in her unholy tears had dried up in her sore eyes, she remarried. Oh, with what a cold heart she hastened with such ease and excessive speed to an incestuous bed!

COMMENTARY: A Missing Father

It was common knowledge in Salem that Brother Harry Winfield was Oscar Hinsley's father. This was an unspoken truth. You see, Rose Hinsley (Oscar's mother) was Brother Winfield's stepdaughter. When it became obvious that Rose was expecting a child, she was asked repeatedly to identify the father. She declined to do so. Her only reply when asked to reveal the father's name was, "Brother Winfield knows who the father is."

However, that was confirmation enough, since Brother Harry Winfield was a notorious philanderer and an unconscionable pedophile. Ironically, he was also a prominent member in one of the local churches. After each misdeed, and perhaps after a few conscience pangs, he would rush to the church to seek re-baptism, foolishly thinking that multi-dipping could mitigate his repeated unspeakable behavior.

Fortunately, Oscar Hinsley grew from childhood to adulthood ostensibly unaffected by his dubious paternity. To this day, I have no knowledge whether Oscar was given any information regarding the circumstances of his birth, but whatever he was told, it did not affect him negatively. He grew up a productive member of the Salem Community.

11. FRIENDSHIP

INTRODUCTION: A Salute to Antigua Girls' High School—Friendship in Brick and Mortar

In 387 B.C., Plato had an idea. He created the first Academy. Plato's idea provided a prototype for our world of academia—a world where lifelong friendships have been formed. Across the globe, the schools of our teen and even pre-teen years have been breeding grounds for enduring friendships. Shakespeare must have had his circle of friends at his grammar school at Stratford-on-Avon. A vital presence in my adolescent life was my high school in the Caribbean. I have used personification and apostrophe in the following tribute to present this school as my maternal friend:

I salute you, Antigua Girls' High School (AGHS)! I recognize you as a guiding force in my formative years. A consequence of the Platonic vision, you emerged and took form as an idea of the Anglican Church. Over one hundred years ago, you burgeoned forth on that hillock on the nether side of that mighty cathedral with its seemingly protective presence. Staffed by pioneers and founders from England, you willingly embraced your mission as follows:

Gather those young girls in and around you.
Nurture them. Instill worthy values in them.
Teach them to be ladies. Encourage them to strive
for excellence in their studies.

We were proud to be AGHS girls. We were special! Our blue uniforms symbolized a Brahmin sisterhood. We had to pass an exam before we were even granted admission to your classrooms, and our families were pleased to provide the tuition to keep us enrolled. You are an integral part of all that you have raised us to be. You taught us discipline. You taught us to love, or like, or at least tolerate one another. We played many friendly games of jacks, volley ball, rounders, net ball, jump rope, and the like within your gates. You taught us to be resilient in defeat. You enveloped us in your maternal embrace until our maturation compelled your release.

With prescience and confidence that we would be successful, you then said,"Go achieve!" And so, we sallied forth to occupy our places in our respective diasporas on this earth. Having achieved, by dint of hard work, we came back to you as doctors, lawyers, professors, teachers, nurses, technologists, economists, and other builders of community—thinkers all.

The bonding—the friendship—is palpable whenever we return home, as we did in 1986 for our centenary celebration when Amelia Charles so eloquently saluted you on our behalf at our convocation in the assembly hall. With gusto, we sang "Lord Behold Us with Thy Blessing," and even as we sang, we were not only friends but also happy, reunited "siblings" seeking and receiving recognition, approval, and blessing from you, our Alma Mater.

Throughout my teenage years, in your classrooms, I formed some of my "golden" lifetime friendships which neither time nor distance will ever diminish. I cherish the memories of those days my friends and I spent traversing the streets of Antigua in innocent, girlhood chatter. I frequently recall the days we sat carefree in the assembly hall or in the dining room, around the piano, singing one song after another: "We Children We Gambol; We Dance in a Ring," "Came You Not from Newcastle," "I'm Lazy Robin," "Rose among the Heather," and many more.

And what about our yearly Carol Service. I was particularly impressed and delighted, each Christmas season, to listen to the thunderous roar of that majestic pipe organ in the cathedral and watch the two sisters who played that instrument with such confidence. Little wonder that I also decided to learn to play the piano and organ. Oh how I wish I could have played the piano then as I do now.

Back then, it would have been my pleasure to have served as one of the musicians in my church that was located across the street from your western gate. It was a small brown church nestled modestly on the leeward side of the cathedral. In the company of some of my AGHS friends, I spent many enjoyable teenage years at this Seventh-day Adventist church in St. John's. I sang in the youth choir and participated in concerts, in evangelistic efforts, and in health programs. We also enjoyed church picnics and hikes planned and supervised by our dedicated youth leader, Mr. Alpha Josiah, who was also our choir director. Wherever we,

AGHS girls, went in the community, your influence was evident in our demeanor and deportment.

Arguably, your overriding achievement is the sturdy, fundamental British education you instilled in us. However, since perfection is elusive and often unattainable in our earthly endeavor, even as I discuss your strengths, it is necessary to comment on one or two flaws as well. At various times in my classes, I did not exert myself. I was sometimes bored and not motivated by some of my teachers. Little wonder that my work was not outstanding during some periods at AGHS. As I look back, I now recognize that some teachers were even more bored and disinterested than I, especially one headmistress from England who consistently yawned at intervals, as she ineffectually passed on one or two frayed bits of knowledge. Fortunately, I later achieved significant academic success in spite of the cold, antagonistic climate that often existed in her classes.

By contrast, let me take this opportunity to recognize publicly the stellar performance of one special teacher at AGHS, Ms. Mary Warrell. I remember being so very sad when she returned to her home in England. From Form 2A, Ms. Warrell has had an indelible impact on my life. It was she who inspired me while I was an adolescent and taught me to write. I frequently recall our English classes under the lofty trees in the schoolyard where we would read and act out a number of Shakespeare's plays including "A Midsummer Night's Dream," "As You Like It," "Macbeth," "The Merchant of Venice," "Julius Caesar," and others. She also introduced us to Perseus, Theseus, Jason, as well as the other Argonauts, and we read and understood the works of many poets. Those were delightful classes in which Ms. Warrell often asked me to read my papers aloud, and I was proud to receive a number of prizes for my work. I wish it were possible to say thanks to Ms. Warrell in person, but failing that, my appreciation is recorded here.

Actually, my indebtedness goes farther back to Mr. Anderson Archibald, my very first English teacher at New Winthorpes Elementary School. Mr. Archibald laid the foundation for all that I achieved in Ms. Warrell's classes. It was he who first taught me, in English classes, to put words together to create effective visual imagery. He taught my class a variety of subjects, from botany to math, and did so with dexterity and brilliance.

Finally, I would be remiss if I did not say a word or two about Mrs. Agnes Jeffrey, my English teacher in Form 6B at the Antigua Grammar School. She was a good teacher who did all she could to motivate us. I truly regret that I did not take my studies seriously at that juncture in my life. I remember that I was one of the students she asked to leave her classroom one day because we had not read *Emma*, though she had given us more than an adequate number of days to do so. For some reason, Jane Austen did not beckon me then as she does today. I often wish it were possible to apologize to Mrs. Jeffrey and tell her thanks for her words of encouragement and for being patient and kind. I will always be grateful to her for believing in me.

Surely, the word "friendship" conjures up pictures of cherished days at AGHS. The great days we spent as "sisters" far outnumbered the unpleasant ones. It is true that endemic to sibling coexistence is carping criticism, bullying, and sometimes downright meanness, all of which I encountered at AGHS. It is common knowledge that children can be cruel to one another. I am pleased to recall, however, that at AGHS, the girls who were mean and unfriendly to me were usually the non-achievers. They were also few and could easily be ignored. So, once more, thank you, Antigua Girls' High School for the enduring impact you have made on my life.

Since My Dear Soul Was Mistress

Since my dear soul was mistress of her choice
And could of men distinguish, her election
Hath sealed thee for herself. For thou hast been
As one in suffering all that suffers nothing,
A man that fortune's buffets and rewards
Hast taken with equal thanks. And blest are those
Whose blood and judgment are so well commingled
That they are not a pipe for fortune's finger
To sound what stop she please. Give me that man
That is not passion's slave, and I will wear him
In my heart's core—aye, in my heart of heart,
As I do thee.
(*Hamlet* 3. 2. 68-78)

PARAPHRASE

Since I allowed my soul (my heart) to guide me in selecting a bosom friend from among my comrades, she (i.e. my soul) has chosen you and set you apart from all others, for you have confronted all things without murmuring. You are a man who accepted misfortunes and rewarding experiences equally. And blessed are those people whose disposition and judgment are so well balanced that they are not like a wind instrument playing many different tunes, over which they have no control. Show me the man who is not a slave to his passions, and I will take him to my bosom (i.e. I will shower him with affection). Yes, I will enfold him in my heart as I have done to you.

Is All the Counsel that We Two Have Shared

Is all the counsel that we two have shared,
The sister's vows, the hours that we have spent,

When we have chid the hasty-footed time
For parting us—oh, is it all forgot?
All school days' friendship, childhood innocence?
We, Hermia, like two artificial gods,
Have with our needles created both one flower,
Both on one sampler, sitting on one cushion,
Both warbling of one song, both in one key—
As if our hands, our sides, voices, and minds
Had been incorporate. So we grew together,
Like to a double cherry, seeming parted
But yet a union in partition—
Two lovely berries molded on one stem
So, with two seeming bodies, but one heart,
Two of the first, like coats in heraldry,
Due but to one, and crowned with one crest.
And will you rent our ancient love asunder,
To join with men in scorning your poor friend?
(*A Midsummer Night's Dream* 3. 2. 198-216)

PARAPHRASE

Is all the confidence that both of us have shared forgotten? Are the promises we made to each other as sisters no longer meaningful? What about the hours we spent together, all the while cursing time for moving so swiftly and forcing us to be separated? Have you forgotten all of this? Do you remember the bond of friendship we formed as school girls, during our childhood innocence? Hermia, you and I like two artistic geniuses embroidered the same flower on the same piece of embroidery, sitting on one cushion, both of us singing the same song in the same key—as if our hands, our sides, our voices, and our minds were in one body. And so, we grew up together like a cherry with twin sections which seem to be separated but are in fact joined. Like two lovely berries nurtured on one stem, we seemed to have two bodies but we shared a single heart like the coat of arms of husband and wife merged into one. So tell me, how could you destroy the bond we established since childhood by joining with men to mock your poor friend?

Antonio, I Am Married to a Wife

Antonio, I am married to a wife
Which is as dear to me as life itself,
But life itself, my wife, and all the world
Are not with me esteemed above thy life.
I would lose all, aye, sacrifice them all
Here to this devil, to deliver you.
(*The Merchant of Venice* 4. 1. 282-87)

PARAPHRASE

Antonio, I have a wife who is as precious to me as life itself. However, my life, my wife's life, and the whole world are not of greater worth than your life. I would give up everything; yes, I would sacrifice all I own in this world to this devil in order to rescue you.

COMMENTARY: Early Friendship—My Adolescent Family Life in Montserrat

Abundant praise goes posthumously to my mother, Mary Elizabeth Buntin, for the warm, friendly environment she created in our home when we were growing up in the island of Montserrat. She worked tirelessly to provide our daily necessities, skillfully balancing the role of mother and friend. She got married early, at nineteen. My father was her first and only "Love."

Travel back with me several decades. On a particular Tuesday evening, the people of Salem held their collective breath in anticipation, only to release it when they heard that, for the tenth time, my mother had given birth to yet another girl. Instead of the boy she had been praying for, without any apology, I had put in my appearance. Perhaps there and then, with a touch of exasperation, she decided to try one last time. Fortunately, two years later, a little boy arrived.

    I am hesitant to believe that any mother has worked as hard to rear her children as my mother did to rear us. We were her pride and joy. She was a multi-talented housewife with unflagging energy. Chief among her innate skills was her sewing. Being an accomplished seamstress, without benefit of sewing classes, she designed and produced many dresses (bridals among them), pants, shirts, jackets, and suits (even three-piece men's suits). I often wonder how she did it! There were many nights when she watched us sleep while she worked on through the early hours of the following day to complete an order due later that day. And yet she found time for gardening. She could wield a hoe with the best among gardeners, as she sought to put in the ground anything that would grow to provide food for us.

    Actually, she provided food for many other children in the neighborhood. Several children who were hungry, displaced, or abused at home would hang around our house, and my mother would divide whatever we were eating and feed them. Food was certainly not abundant, and space was limited, and yet, my mother adopted one or two of those children and brought them home to live with us. My mother was a veritable Angel of Mercy. In ministering to the displaced, she did not stop at children. I remember an old man who returned home penniless from Cuba and an old woman, also penniless, homeless, and friendless. My mother took them both in and shared whatever we had with them without any form of recompense.

    I now reflect on some of the other things my mother did in her valiant effort to provide for us. She was a shoemaker. It is with a smile that I recall the fact that she not only mended our shoes, but she also bought leather and made her own creations to stretch the dollars. Back then I was not, but today, I am proud to say that I have worn one or two of what I now call Mary Elizabeth Originals! She could also dabble in cement. Any construction worker, who agreed to do any work at our house, knew that he had to work not "for" her but "with" her. For instance, when she decided that it was necessary to add one or two rooms to our house, there she was--handling the bricks, helping to arrange and provide guidance in all aspects of the construction. Not even in sickness (hers or ours) was her resourcefulness depleted. She would nurse us or nurse herself back to health in less than no time. If any mother earned the name of Phoenix, mine certainly did. I always think of her whenever I read King Solomon's profile of the exemplary woman. He must have met my mother:

> Who can find a virtuous woman? for her price is far above rubies. The heart of her husband doth safely trust in her, so that he shall have no need of spoil. She will do him good and not evil all the days of her life. She seeketh wool, and flax, and worketh willingly with her hands. She is like the merchants' ships; she bringeth her food from afar. She riseth also while it is yet night, and giveth meat to her household, and a portion to her maidens. She considereth a field, and buyeth it: with the fruit of her hands she planteth a vineyard. She girdeth her loins with strength, and stengtheneth her arms. She perceiveth that her merchandise is good: her candle goeth not out by night. She layeth her hands to the spindle, and her hands hold the distaff. She stretcheth out her hand to the poor; yea, she reacheth forth her hands to the needy. . . . Strength and honour are her clothing; and she shall rejoice in time to come. She openeth her mouth with wisdom; and in her tongue is the law of kindness. She looketh

well to the ways of her household, and eateth not the bread of idleness. Her children arise up, and call her blessed; her husband also, and he praiseth her. Many daughters have done virtuously, but thou excellest them all. Favour is deceitful, and beauty is vain: but a woman that feareth the Lord, she shall be praised. Give her of the fruit of her hands; and let her own works praise her in the gates.
(*Proverbs* 31: 10-20; 25-31)

Quite possibly, my father did not realize the priceless gem he married. I have said thank you to my mother several times in the past; I wish it were possible for me to say thank you just one more time.

In addition to all that I have described, I can say that my mother deftly doubled as mother and teacher. In our daily communication, we had to watch our language because we were not allowed to speak so-called "broken" English. She gathered her children around her, and with the centripetal force of a magnet, she kept us connected not only to her but also to one another. To keep us from being embroiled in youthful conflicts at school and elsewhere, our mother and father would tell us repeatedly, "You don't need any friends. There are many of you right here in this house, so you have all the friends you need."

My father was a far more stringent advocate of these principles than even my mother. We were, therefore, more watchful of our behavior when he was home from Antigua than when he was away. A self-educated man, he usually sat in his favorite chair, surrounded by many books, devouring as much knowledge as he could beyond the basic education he had gleaned in school. We learned about far away lands because of the information he usually shared with us. He was a poet. He wrote many lyrical, didactic, and patriotic poems especially about Montserrat. He was a musician. He wrote the words and music for many songs primarily with themes about the Caribbean.

And so, we grew up doing everything together. We were a happy band of nine—eight girls and one boy (twin girls died in infancy). With our mother, we were ten against the world. We lived in a white concrete house situated on a hill. When we stood in our living room and looked to the East, in the distance, we could see the towering majesty of the mountain, bathed in blue and white, as its peak seemed to touch the clouds. Turning immediately to the West, also from the living room, it was a pleasure to watch the blue waters of the Atlantic Ocean stretching for miles and miles in the distance. Each day, we would watch as the ships emerged, carrying their cargo and passengers, and then disappeared behind the surrounding cliffs.

From time to time, my father would come home on one of those ships, carrying a treasure trove of books for us to read. He would read with us and to us. I remember vividly the first time I ever heard of the Titanic. I was about seven years old when my father gathered us all around him to read from a big book with the narrative and colored pictures of that disaster. He told us the names of all the millionaires that perished that night along with over a thousand other passengers. We saw the iceberg. We saw the band members who played nonstop until the ship sank. He showed us the music of the hymns the band played, and he taught us the tunes of the hymns we didn't know. I remember being deeply depressed to hear of the plight of those people.

Fortunately, in those early days, many other activities brought joy instead of sadness. We often played games such as hide and seek, ring a rosey, pass the secret, jump rope, and many more. We also enjoyed playing with our cousins. Our treks to gather wood, almonds, mangoes, guavas, sour sops, bananas, and coconuts were particularly exhilarating. We would walk a few miles from home, singing, laughing, and telling jokes. When we reached our destination—the neighboring woods or our land extension with fruit trees—we would fill our bellies on the spot with the sweet, yellow nectar of the mangoes and the cooling, refreshing coconut water and jelly. Then we would load up our containers with our booty to be taken home.

Some stay-at-home days, when I was alone in the backyard, I would sneak into my mother's vegetable garden and hide in the cabbage patch among the cabbage and pumpkin leaves, while I devoured several of her ripe tomatoes. And, of course, my brother and I made many trips between meals to a plum tree that grew on the northern side of our house. Those were the days when we enjoyed our own organic produce.

Sometimes, we all went to a nearby river for part of the day. While my older sisters washed a load of clothes, we younger ones would stick our toes in the crystal, clear water and watch the playful fish swim to and fro. As we giggled and frolicked, we seemed to have amused the fish just as they had entertained us. After a while, we would go for a dip in the cool, soothing shallow part of the river.

Sundays were musical days at our home in Montserrat. Each Sunday, all our chores—whether cleaning, washing, cooking, ironing, sewing—were done while we listened to the tunes being played on an old phonograph that was one of our prized possessions. The melodies filled the rooms of our house and spilled onto the street just outside our house. As we worked, we sang along with tunes such as "The Bells of St. Mary," "Casey Jones," "Listen to the Mockingbird," "Let Me Call You Sweetheart," and many more. I believe we had the only phonograph for miles around, so some of our neighbors gathered in our home and just outside the front door to listen and sing along with us. I recall the years I spent in that cheerful, friendly atmosphere.

However, No Period of My Life in Montserrat Was as Enjoyable as Christmas!

Christmas fever started for us Montserratian kids from November fifth, Guy Fawkes Day, when the demise of Guy Fawkes and his cohorts is celebrated in British territories. Back then, we would carry lighted torches to commemorate Guy Fawkes' failure to set fire to the British Parliament several centuries ago. This is the typical scene on the night of each November fifth when I was a child in Salem: A blanket of darkness covers Salem not long after sunset. Then lights spring up one after another from all over the village—from east, west, south, north. These are moving lights—men, women, and children carrying pieces of burning, flaming inner tire tube, heading for the central meeting place in front of Mr. Walker's store. There is much laughter, joking, socializing, carousing, and eating before the gathering disperses.

After Guy Fawkes' night, Christmas always seemed to take an age to arrive, but eventually it would be Christmas Eve. This was the main Christmas preparation day in Montserrat. This was the day that the excitement rose and became almost intolerable for us, kids in Salem. My mother usually baked cakes, tarts, pies, and cassava bread, and prepared delicious ginger beer and sorrel drinks. At this time of year, there was usually a mixing and mingling of satisfying sights, smells, and sounds. We were always surrounded by golden brown cakes and breads as well as juicy brown roasted legs of lamb and other meat especially codfish. Each dish exuded an intoxicating aroma.

During this bustling preparation, we would sing the popular Christmas carols, and the joy of Christmas would saturate the scene. Ironically, one of the Christmas carols we usually sang is "In the Bleak Mid Winter," and our hearts were usually warmed and made more joyful when we recognized the stark contrast between the Christmas we were singing about and the one that was our reality. In the islands, we had no knowledge of "winter" or "frosty winds" or "snow." Christmas was all warmth, sunshine, friendship, and happiness. To complete the beauty of the domestic scene, my sisters usually made gorgeous, elaborate, natural-looking artificial flowers--roses, lilies, daisies, carnations, tulips, orchids, and the like—as well as garlands, banners, and fly catchers. The neighbors would often come to visit our home and compliment us on our beautiful decorations.

Finally, night would envelop the scene on Christmas Eve, and though we kids tried to fight sleep, we would eventually drift off only to be awakened around four o'clock on Christmas morning by the rousing, cheering singing of the carolers. "While Shepherds Watched Their Flocks by Night," "Hark the Herald Angels Sing," "O Come All Ye Faithful"—these were some of the favorites of the carolers. But my favorite was "Good King Wenceslas." Each time they sang the first line of this carol, I was always aware that the Good King was not the only one spying on the "feast" that would be devoured come daylight. And when they sang, "Silent Night Holy Night, All Is Calm. . ." I thought, not true! I was anything but "calm," having made atleast three disappointing trips throughout the night to where our stockings were hanging, only to see (actually to feel) that Father Christmas had not yet visited our house. What's keeping him, I wondered. I bet it's Sarah Smith at the end of the road. She always has so many toys! He's taking extra time to fill her stocking, I bet.

Just before morning light, I would make one last trip to where the stockings were hung. Finally! Hurrah! He came! He came! I often thought, "Joy to the World," indeed, just as the carolers had sung! I would then rush back to wake up the others and tell them the good news, but not before feeling each stocking and trying to guess what was inside. I remember my very first precious doll. I felt her before I even saw her. Her soft, chubby body was tucked between mounds of candy in an extra large stocking that year.

Before we ate breakfast, as usual, we were allowed to raid our stockings and enjoy our booty courtesy of the Man from the North Pole. As I played with my doll, I heard the sound of a mouth organ (harmonica) coming from my sisters' end of the room. Boisterous notes from a horn, a flute, a drum and noises from squeaking toys, crackling toys, and toys that tumbled and rumbled soon erupted in such volume that even my doll seemed tempted to cover her ears to shut out the cacophonous sounds of Christmas. By the way, it was only later, years later, that I discovered that it was my sister in America who was, indeed, our Father (Mother) Christmas, sending stocking stuffers and so much more each year. How fortunate we were to have her. Every year, after that first Christmas day, we celebrated one full week of Christmas until New Year's Day. Each day, there were masquerades, costumed revelers, parades, eating, drinking, and dancing in the streets to steel drums, fifes, and other instruments.

Arguably, the most exciting aspect of Christmas in Salem was the Bull. He was a giant of a man, a Goliath, who dressed each Christmas in a costume to replicate a big, black, angry, bloodthirsty bull that was menacing from head to foot in appearance and demeanor. His entire body was covered in black leather and hairy burlap. The skin of a real bull covered his large chest. On his head, he balanced two huge horns that were thicker and longer than those of any Texan longhorn bull. On his size forty feet, were enormous black leather boots that extended above his knees.

With each stride, he crushed the pebbles and shook the earth beneath. A long tail trailed behind him, and in his hand he carried a long pitchfork. Anyone who dared to look him in the face would see the most hideous, twisted, contorted, hairy mask made of black leather with red streaks (simulating blood). A pair of savage eyes lurked beneath surrounding tufts of hair and burlap. Like Medusa, the Gorgon, that face could almost turn to stone anyone who dared to look.

There was no child, no woman, and perhaps no man who was not terrified by that marauding Bull. Many of the men who faced him did so with feigned temerity. I believe even his mother must have shivered involuntarily when she saw her son transformed as the Bull each Christmas. Like a real ferocious bull, he would grimace, roar, and lunge at the few souls brave enough to encounter him. For most of us, the joy of Christmas reached a paradoxical crescendo each Christmas Day as we peeped like scared mice from behind shuttered doors to see our greatest attraction—our greatest source of fear yet excitement—striding like a colossus past our houses. What we dreaded most was the possibility of turning a corner somewhere in the neighborhood and finding ourselves face to face with the Bull. If this situation ever occurred, we would experience fear-induced paralysis for a split second, and then we would take to our heels with the Bull in lumbering pursuit. Our fear simply boosted his adrenalin and his resolve to terrify us all.

Eventually, inevitably, adulthood encroached on this childhood idyllic scene and brought in its ravaging wake separation in all its forms: travel and goodbyes, jobs and other responsibilities, different homes, marriages, children, different lifestyles, different values, disagreements, even problems and conflicts, as well as sickness and death. However, in spite of the complications of adulthood, nothing can erase either our early memories or our familial bond.

12. DREAMS

INTRODUCTION

From ancient to modern mankind, dreams have always mystified us. What is the cause of this phenomenon? Why do we dream? Are dreams the result of our over-active subconscious taking control while our bodies rest, as Freud contends? Isn't it strange and wonderful that we can explore foreign lands, conquer any foe, achieve the unachievable, and be embroiled in irrational, undecipherable, even dangerous situations while fast asleep? And isn't it great that we can awake untouched, unscathed even after horrifying nightmares? We, humans, have always sought to put meaning to our dreams. Pharaoh and Nebuchadnezzar couldn't rest until Joseph and Daniel (respectively) interpreted their dreams (*Genesis* 41 and *Daniel* 2).

And how many of us have seen, in our dreams, something similar to the proverbial "writing on the wall," as Belshazzar did, and received our own cautionary version of "Mene mene tekel upharsin" (*Daniel* 5)? Shakespeare reminds us that Julius Caesar would not have been murdered in the capitol on that fateful day if only he had stayed at home, as his wife begged him to do, after she had foreseen his death in her dream. Sometimes, our dreams descend to the realm of nightmare, and we are grateful when someone awakens us.

I believe that among the panoply of dreams we humans dream every night is reflected our quest, our perennial need, to find friendship. I mean true, unadulterated, unconditional friendship. I mean the kind of friend who is almost an extension of one's body, a friend to whom a person can lay bare his or her soul without a moment's hesitation. True friendship is indeed as precious as gold and almost as rare. In many instances, we use the word "friend" too readily, too lightly, too loosely usually as a misnomer for acquaintance. Unfortunately, we often encounter true friends only in dreams and must eventually "wake, and find nothing," as Shakespeare puts it.

Poor Wretches that Depend

              Poor wretches that depend
On greatness' favor dream as I have done,
Wake, and find nothing.
(*Cymbeline* 5. 4. 127-29)

PARAPHRASE

Desperate souls who hope to improve their lot and even achieve greatness resort to dreaming as I have done. However, we are destined to awaken and find that there is no substance to our dreams.

Calpurnia Here, My Wife, Stays Me at Home

Caesar: Calpurnia here, my wife, stays me at home.
 She dreamt tonight she saw my statue,
 Which like a fountain with a hundred spouts
 Did run pure blood, and many lusty Romans
 Came smiling and did bathe their hands in it.
 And these does she apply for warnings and portents
 And evils imminent; and on her knee
 Hath begged that I will stay at home today.

Brutus: This dream is all amiss interpreted.
 It was a vision fair and fortunate.
 Your statue spouting blood in many pipes,
 In which so many smiling Romans bathed,
 Signifies that from you great Rome shall suck
 Reviving blood; and that great men shall press
 For tinctures, stains, relics, and cognizance.
 This by Calpurnia's dream is signified.
 (*Julius Caesar* 2. 2. 75-90)

PARAPHRASE

Caesar: My wife, Calpurnia, has asked me to stay at home. Tonight she dreamt she saw my statue in the shape of a fountain with a hundred spouts from which pure blood gushed, and many robust Romans flippantly washed their hands in it. She regards this dream as an omen, as a sign of impending tragedy. Therefore on her knees, she begged me to remain home today.

Brutus: This dream has been given the wrong interpretation. It is a good dream, one that foretells your good fortune. The fact that so many smiling Romans bathed in the blood pouring from your statue means that you will be the agent to infuse new life into dying Rome; it means that great Romans will jostle one another to be marked with your blood, and these blood stains will be prized souvenirs, relics, and emblems. This is what Calpurnia's dream means.

COMMENTARY: My Knight and Amorland—a Dream Realized

There is another kind of dream, one akin to hope, to aspiration. This is the kind of dreaming we do when we are wide awake, the kind of dreaming whose fulfillment is often so elusive. This is the type of dream that would transport the dreamer to another world, another life, if it were to materialize. Chrystal Gayle's recording titled "When I Dream" captures the essence of this idea: the fact that we may derive pleasure from doing a hundred-and-one things with a hundred-and-one different people without ever finding that special person "somewhere out there" who can provide the proverbial helium to transport us beyond the rainbow, beyond the moon, and enable us to occupy a land that rises far above all things mundane.

For years, I dreamed and hoped to find a mate with whom I could recapture and keep the happy, idyllic life I lost in childhood. I wanted to meet someone who could make every day "Christmas" similar to the Christmases I enjoyed as a child in Montserrat. I dreamed of finding someone who would complete my life in adulthood as my mother completed my life in childhood. All right, yes. I wanted someone to "spoil" me. Was that asking too much? I didn't think so. It is said that good things (and I might add "good mates") come to those who wait, and I'll add "and pray." The "golden" person I sought exists in the daydreams of many but is destined to become reality for only a fortunate few.

I therefore continued my search for years, half hoping, half despairing. My quest was for someone with whom I could form an undying friendship, someone to whom I could repeat Ruth's words of unwavering commitment: "Whither thou goest, I will go; wherever thou lodgest I will lodge. . . " (*Ruth* 1: 16-18). I intended to search until I found someone to whom I could repeat the beautiful words of the following sonnet that Elizabeth Barrett Browning (1806-61) wrote for her husband:

> How do I love thee? Let me count the ways.
> I love thee to the depth and breadth and height
> My soul can reach, when feeling out of sight
> For the ends of Being and Ideal Grace.
> I love thee to the level of everyday's
> Most quiet need, by sun and candlelight.
> I love thee freely, as men strive for Right;
> I love thee purely, as they turn from Praise.
> I love thee with the passion put to use
> In my old griefs, and with my childhood's faith.
> I love thee with a love I seemed to lose
> With my lost saints,-- I love thee with the breath,
> Smiles, tears, of all my life!—and, if God choose,
> I shall but love thee better after death.

I hoped to find someone with whom I could share a "single soul dwelling in two bodies," as Aristotle puts it.

Year after year, I continued to dream, and all the while I knew that the person in my dreams was identical to the one George Eliot (1819-80) so eloquently describes here:

> Oh, the comfort, the inexpressible comfort of feeling safe with a person; having neither to weigh thoughts nor measure words, but to pour them all out, just as they are, chaff and grain together, knowing that a faithful hand will take and sift them, keep what is worth keeping, and then, with the breath of kindness, blow the rest away.

A profile of the person with whom I would find this "safe" habor as described by Eliot was ever present in my mind. But where is he, I asked myself for years. Where will I find someone who shares my interests? Where will I find someone who genuinely enjoys the classical music I enjoy: Chopin's nocturnes, etudes, and polonaises as well as the music of Beethoven, Mozart, Bach, Handel, and the other masters? Where, I asked myself, will I find someone to quote passages from Shakespeare and other famous writers with me? Where will I find someone who will engage in the conjugation and declension of Latin verbs and nouns, respectively, and practice oral French with me, and share other experiences of the good old school days in the islands?

I asked myself, Where will I find someone of a lofty, moral character who is not only academically astute, not only courteous and kind, but one who also deems it his **duty** to take full financial responsibility for all aspects of our home, providing a comfortable lifestyle, including domestic help? Where is that someone, I asked myself, who would laugh when I laugh, cry when I cry, help with day to day mundane chores, and return the love—the care and attention—he receives in full measure?

Above all, I asked myself, Where will I find someone who will have family worship with me, someone who will meditate and pray regularly with me and study the Bible with me? Will that person also enjoy listening to the good old Advent hymns? Will he sit at the piano with me and sing along when I play those hymns at home? With a measure of incredulity I continually asked myself, Where on planet earth does such an exceptional person exist?

Then one day, one auspicious day, God in His beneficence allowed the Prince of my dreams to materialize with all of the sterling qualities I dreamed of and more. Many who have met him share my view of him as a veritable patrician, a knight in shining armor. It is as if Shakespeare also knew him and wrote the following lines to honor him:

> . . . when he shall die,
> Take him and cut him out in little stars,
> And he will make the face of heaven so fine
> That all the world will be in love with night,
> And pay no worship to the garish sun.
> (*Romeo and Juliet* 3. 2. 21-25)

Several years ago, while a friend of mine prepared for her wedding, she asked me to write a poem to mark the occasion. As I gave her request some thought and pondered what to write, a beautiful metaphor unfolded in my mind. What if love were perceived as a place, a country, a haven? I asked myself. All mortals would seek to live there. Even as the idea morphed in my mind, I knew I had to find a good name for this special country. I coined the name "Amorland" from the Latin "amor" (amare—amo, amas, amat, etc.) which means "love." This is the land I occupy. With abundant appreciation, I dedicate this poem to my beloved husband:

Love Is a Country—Amorland: an Ode

Love is a country, Utopian in scope
Where lovers find refuge, where lovers find hope.
There are no immigration laws here, not even one court.
Anyone with a heart can enter this port.
To this great country, millions seek the coveted key:
The sad, the glad, the poor, the rich, the old, the young
All yearn to be free.
So where is this country?
Where must one go
To find the affluence of El Dorado?
Where must one go to find such bliss?
Must one seek the elusive Atlantis?
Where must one travel to find this cherished spot?
Must one seek out the legendary Camelot?
How can one see what great lovers saw
Within the illustrious confines of Shangrila?
So where is this Magic Kingdom, this country without flaw
That provided safe haven for Antony and Cleopatra?
It is any spot on earth that is shared by two.
It could be a mansion, a hut, a ship, or canoe.
If your heart and that of your spouse share the same rhythmic beat,
If your lives are entwined, if your home is a safe retreat,
If your arms give and receive asylum in sickness or in health,
And you are restful, calm, and devoted in poverty or wealth,
Consider yourself a proud citizen of Amorland—the Country of Love—
A place that is blessed by our Father above,
A place where joy and peace abound,
A country that few lovers have actually found.

I feel compelled to close this chapter with an eye-opening quotation from Hugh Walpole (1884-1941):

> The most wonderful of all things in life, I believe, is the discovery of another human being with whom one's relationship has a glowing depth, beauty and joy. . . . This inner progressiveness of love between two human beings is a most marvelous thing. It cannot be found by looking for it or by passionately wishing for it. It is a sort of Divine accident.

I prefer to call it Divine intervention that comes as a consequence of prayer.

My knight and his motorized steed

I often enjoy the soothing and refreshing
effect of water under a clear sky.

13. SUICIDE

INTRODUCTION

Too often in this world when life seems meaningless, when problems assail, when each episode seems to connect with the destructive force of a battering ram, suicide is seen by some as the only viable solution. For thousands of years, suicide has enabled many to turn their backs on the world without laboring to conquer what they considered unconquerable. For centuries, mankind has used suicide as an escape, as a problem-solving tool.

The noble Romans deemed it honorable to fall on their swords instead of enduring defeat and captivity. The samurai warriors of Japan, in abeyance to their honor code, ripped their abdomens open with daggers or knives (hara kiri) rather than face disgrace or death by other hands. In

World War II, the Japanese Kamikaze corps, in their explosives-laden aircrafts, didn't hesitate to fly suicidal missions into enemy targets in an effort to achieve victory at all cost.

Too many people today are also resorting to suicide as a problem solver, albeit a dubious one. Suicides are rare in Antigua and Montserrat, but everyday, in some part of the world, there are suicides. Surely, we wish that such a desperate, dreadful act would be on the decline, but not so. The proliferation of suicides, even before the world economy deteriorated, is astounding. Almost everyday we hear of yet another murder-suicide. Just yesterday, a father somewhere in Florida killed his wife and five children and then killed himself. Another father did the same thing the week before, stating in his suicide note that he did not want his family to suffer after his death because of their depleted income.

Even ostensibly successful people resort to suicide as an escape, to make a point, or to solve a problem. A few years ago, a popular politician in Miami, who was under scrutiny for one reason or other, shot himself in the head in the lobby of the Miami Herald Building. And, of course, we all have heard of Dr. Kevorkian's mission to "assist" seniors who wish to exit this life.

The sad fact is that our young people—teenagers and even pre-teens—are also committing suicide, mistakenly viewing this act as an escape or as a means of making a statement to family, to friends, to the world. Even as I write, I just heard a radio psychologist say, "I don't think there's a teenager who has not considered suicide." What a sad thought! Recently, we heard the tragic story of the student at a University in New York who jumped to his death in order to end his problems. But horror of all horrors, the most disturbing news of current suicides surfaced in the media a few hours ago. A seven-year-old boy somewhere in a Florida foster care facility hanged himself. How is this possible? It is indeed a nerve-shattering realization that even babies are committing suicide.

Shakespeare cautions all who are so inclined to stop and consider that the after life is unknown territory. The implication is that it may be worse than the current life. Above all, he reminds us (in the second excerpt below) that suicide is a sin, and I might add, one which must remain unpardoned since no one can ask for forgiveness after death.

To Be, or Not To Be—That Is the Question

To be, or not to be—that is the question.
Whether 'tis nobler in the mind to suffer
The slings and arrows of outrageous fortune,
Or take arms against a sea of troubles
And by opposing end them. To die, to sleep—
No more, and by a sleep to say we end
The heartache and the thousand natural shocks
That flesh is heir to. 'Tis a consummation
Devoutly to be wished. To die, to sleep,
To sleep—perchance to dream. Aye, there's the
    rub,
For in that sleep of death what dreams may come
When we have shuffled off this mortal coil
Must give us pause. There's the respect
That makes calamity of so long life.
For who would bear the whips and scorns of time,
The oppressor's wrong, the proud man's contumely
The pangs of despised love, the law's delay,
The insolence of office and the spurns
That patient merit of the unworthy takes,
When he himself might his quietus make
With a bare bodkin? Who would fardels bear,
To grunt and sweat under a weary life,
But that the dread of something after death,
The undiscovered country from whose bourn

No traveler returns, puzzles the will,
And makes us rather bear those ills we have
Than fly to others that we know not of?
Thus conscience does make cowards of us all,
And thus the native hue of resolution
Is sicklied o'er with the pale cast of thought,
And enterprises of great pitch and moment
With this regard their currents turn awry
And lose the name of action.
(*Hamlet* 3. 1. 56-88)

PARAPHRASE

To continue living or to put an end to life is a decision we sometimes have to make. We sometimes find ourselves pondering whether it is wiser or more rewarding to endure the darts or blows of cruel fate (destiny) or whether it is better to confront the endless ordeals that come our way and tackle them and put an end to them. But consider Death! Endless sleep! No more pain! In a final, irrevocable sleep, we could drown all heartaches and the innumerable trials and tribulations that we as mortals are subject to. That is a tempting solution to pain and sorrow—one to be craved. How pleasant it would be to die! To sleep! To sleep and perhaps to dream! But here is where the complication lies, for in the sleep of death the dreams we may have after we have cast off this mortal life must cause us to stop and think. There is a sound argument that it is a calamity to have to live a very long life, because who would welcome the typical adverse circumstances in life: the oppressor's persecution, the arrogant man's insulting behavior, the torture of rejected love, the delay in legal matters, the insolent behavior of government officials, and the insults which worthy (good) people have to endure patiently as the unworthy people dish them out. In the midst of all this, an individual could simply, quietly exit this life with the help of his or her dagger. Who would bear burdens and grunt and sweat in an oppressive life if it were not for fear of the after life—the fear or reluctance to enter that undiscovered region from whose boundary no traveler ever returns? It is this fear of the unknown that cripples the determination to put an end to the life we know and makes us choose to endure the troubles we have in this life rather than rush to experience others about which we know nothing. Therefore, the uncertainty that surrounds the after life makes us cowardly and reluctant to act. Consequently, the natural urge to end all is undermined by our thoughts (i.e., our analysis of the situation) with the result that great enterprises (i.e., the great plans we made) are laid aside and forgotten.

Oh, that This Too Too Solid Flesh Would Melt

Oh, that this too too solid flesh would melt,
Thaw, and resolve itself into a dew!
Or that the Everlasting had not fixed
His cannon 'gainst self-slaughter! Oh, God! God!
How weary, stale, flat, and unprofitable
Seem to me all the uses of this world!
Fie on 't, oh, fie! 'Tis an unweeded garden,
That grows to seed, things rank and gross in nature
Possess it merely.
(*Hamlet* 1. 2. 129-37)

PARAPHRASE

Oh, if only this body of mine were not so perfectly solid! If only it could dissolve and disappear! Or if only God Almighty (Jehovah) had not established a law against suicide! Oh God! How tiresome, stale, boring, and unprofitable life seems to be! How unfortunate! Life is an unweeded garden that is overgrown with weeds. Wild, coarse, unhealthy plants have taken over life's garden entirely.

Then Is It Sin?

>Then is it sin
>To rush into the secret house of death
>Ere death dare come to us?
>(*Antony and Cleopatra* 4. 15. 80-82)

PARAPHRASE

Is it a sin to rush to death's secluded domain hurriedly, prematurely, through suicide, before death comes to us by some other means?***

*****NOTE:** Shakespeare's obvious answer to this question is yes.

It Is Silliness To Live When To Live Is Torment

>It is silliness to live when to live is torment,
>and then have we a prescription to die when death
>is our physician.
>(*Othello* 1. 3. 309-11)

PARAPHRASE

It makes very little sense to continue living when life is torture, knowing that we have a prescription for death which brings balm or healing (i.e. suicide).***

***NOTE:** Through the voices of his characters, Shakespeare often argued both sides of an issue.

Even by the Rule of That Philosophy

Even by the rule of that philosophy
By which I did blame Cato for the death
Which he did give himself—I know not how,
But I do find it cowardly and vile,
For fear of what might fall, so to prevent
The time of life—arming myself with patience
To stay the providence of some high powers
That govern us below.
(*Julius Caesar* 5. 1. 101-108)

PARAPHRASE

In keeping with my philosophy of life, I blame Cato for committing suicide. I don't know why, but I consider it cowardly and vile for someone to commit suicide because he or she dreads what the future holds. On the contrary, arming myself with patience, I choose to await or abide by the plan that the superhuman forces that govern our lives have designed for me.

Why, He That Cuts off Twenty Years

Why, he that cuts off twenty years of life
Cuts off so many years of fearing death.
(*Julius Caesar* 3. 1. 101-02)

PARAPHRASE

Anyone who shortens his or her life by twenty years spares himself or herself twenty years of agonizing about eventual death.

Here, Here Will I Remain

    Here, here will I remain
With worms that are thy chambermaids. Oh, here
Will I set up my everlasting rest,
And shake the yoke of inauspicious stars
From this world-wearied flesh. Eyes, look your last!
Arms, take your last embrace! And lips, O you
The doors of breath, seal with a righteous kiss
A dateless bargain to engrossing death!
Come, bitter conduct, come, unsavory guide!
Thou desperate pilot, now at once run on
The dashing rocks thy seasick weary bark.
Here's to my love! O true apothecary!
Thy drugs are quick. Thus with a kiss I die.
(*Romeo and Juliet* 5. 3. 108-20)

PARAPHRASE

I will stay here with worms that are your attendants. Oh, I will set up my final resting place here and shake the streak of bad luck that has trailed this body which is weary with the world. Eyes, take a last look! Arms, embrace her for the last time! And lips, through which breath is emitted, seal with a sacred kiss an everlasting bargain with all-encompassing death. Come to me, you bitter, unwholesome instrument of death. As a desperate pilot runs his storm-tossed ship on the rocks, convey this tired frame to its demise. Here's to my love! What quick, potent poison! With a kiss I die.

COMMENTARY: A Caribbean Incident—a View from the Other Side of Suicide

An incident that took place on a hot, muggy Sunday afternoon in Salem caused me to arrive at the firm belief that many who resort to suicide do so unwillingly. Further, quite possibly, in the few minutes before they lose consciousness, many wish they could change their minds. It must be a terrifying moment for even the most intrepid among us to see the gaping cavernous jaws of death open to separate those who approach from the realm of the known to the unknown.

One seemingly uneventful day in Salem when I was about nine years old, I heard a sudden commotion outside my house. Some people were running in the footpath that led south, and others were hurrying across pasture land, heading in the same direction. My curiosity got the better of me, and so I joined the crowd even without my mother's permission. Seeing that she was occupied elsewhere and unaware of the people hurrying by, I decided I would let her know what was happening after I found out.

I soon recognized that the crowd was headed in the direction of Mr. Samuel's house. He led a reclusive life, his sole companion being his faithful dog which was barking furiously, agitated by the gathering crowd. I tried to get as close to the house as possible, but the adults were milling around, and they kept me at bay.

After some time, I saw four strong, burly men emerge from the house carrying Mr. Samuel who was draped in a sheet from head to toe. As they laid him in the bed of a pickup truck, I saw Dr. Richards climb into the truck and sit beside Mr. Samuel, and the truck drove off.

Eventually, as the crowd dispersed, only then did someone see fit to tell me what had transpired in Mr. Samuel's house. I discovered that Mr. Samuel had tried to kill himself. He had decided to commit suicide by cutting his own throat with a knife. But here's the funny part. Sorry, not funny! "Strange" is a better word here. The strange fact is that Mr. Samuel had started to cut from the back of his throat, not the front. And the cut was not very deep. Though he had lost some blood, he didn't even lose consciousness. When the men carried him from his house, they took him to the hospital where he received the proper care for his wound.

Even now as I reflect on the incident, I recognize that Mr. Samuel was simply crying out for attention. Perhaps he was sending a message to his neighbors who were not very friendly to him. "Now, they'll be sorry!" he might have said to himself. However, he obviously did not have the heart to take his own life. I find myself wondering how many people who completed the act of suicide had second thoughts moments before the deed was complete.

I often think of a former colleague of mine and wonder if this belated mind change was not his experience. He was an amiable, friendly professor in my department at Miami-Dade College who one day, suddenly, committed suicide. I remember being surprised and bewildered when I heard the news. For days, I was haunted by the realization of this unnecessary loss of life. I found myself imagining that even as he fell (he had thrown himself off a bridge), even while he was in the air hurtling to the ground, I could hear him saying, "My God, what am I doing! What have I done! Please God, reverse the pull of gravity and take me back to the bridge!"

To anyone who may be, at this very moment, pondering the "to be or not to be" question, here is my advice as well as Shakespeare's: "Be!" Give life another chance. Why face eternal damnation, as Shakespeare reminds us, when time brings solutions to most problems? Therefore, keep the Faith, and keep the state of "being" as long as possible.

14. CHILD ABUSE: A VOICE FOR THE INNOCENTS

INTRODUCTION

Child abuse is one of the oldest crimes in the history of planet earth. Throughout the years, in communities in the East, West, North, and South, children have been abducted, starved, sold into slavery and sexual trade, raped, beaten, killed, even massacred. Remember Pharaoh's and Herod's Slaughter of the Innocents thousands of years ago? The question that persists, for which there seems to be no answer, is why would anyone want to hurt those precious, defenseless, harmless human beings? For some reason, their very purity and innocence hold an attraction for perverts and psychopaths.

Unfortunately, Montserrat and Antigua have had their share of sexual, physical, and mental child abusers. Granted the incidents occurred on a smaller scale when I was growing up in the islands than they do in large, metropolitan cities, but in these islands, pedophiles stalked young children as they do in any other community. Mothers and fathers had to be vigilant.

Somewhere in America, virtually every other day, the six o'clock news announces yet another crime against children: either rape, abduction, severe beating, or some other violation including death. Just the other day, somewhere in Alaska, a mother poured hot sauce in her little son's mouth whenever he did not tell the truth, and she also subjected him to cold showers.

Two additional heinous examples of child abuse which occurred in Florida will suffice to show the viciousness of abuse of children and the grotesque crimes perpetrated against them. A couple adopted twins, a boy and a girl. At age nine or ten, the beautiful little girl was beaten to death, her decomposing body found in an abandoned vehicle. Her brother was dowsed with some flammable substance and was severely burned. Shortly after this sad story surfaced, the bodies of another brother and sister were found stuffed in suitcases floating in a canal somewhere in Florida. These are heart-wrenching incidents indeed.

Those among us who are students of English history know that there was wide-scale abuse and exploitation of young children during the Industrial Revolution (c. 1750-1850), in the congested London factory towns, when small children were stuffed in the dark, soot-filled chimneys, commissioned to sweep them clean. So many children died as a result of lung diseases, exposure, and starvation.

The English poet, William Blake, has chronicled the plight of these children in his poetic collection entitled *Songs of Innocence* (1789). The poem titled "The Chimney Sweeper" is one of the best known in this collection. Here is an excerpt:

> When my mother died I was very young,
> And my father sold me while yet my tongue
> Could scarcely cry "'weep! 'weep! 'weep!
>   ''weep!"
> So your chimneys I sweep, & in soot I
>   sleep.
> ....
> As Tom was a-sleeping, he had such a
>   sight!
> That thousands of sweepers, Dick, Joe,
>   Ned, & Jack,
> Were all of them lock'd up in coffins of
>   black.
> And by came an Angel who had a bright
>   key,
> And he open'd the coffins & set them all
>   free;
> Then down a green plain leaping, laugh-
>   ing, they run,
> And wash in a river, and shine in the Sun.

What about Charles Dickens? No other writer has portrayed the dilemma of the young orphans in England as effectively as he has done in his immortal classics: *Oliver Twist, David Copperfield, and Great Expectations.* In the public charity schools and workhouses, on the treacherous streets of London, or living with uncaring relatives, these children endured daily abuse and endangerment.

Shakespeare has also been a loud voice for the Innocents. Abuse, violation, or destruction of children is a recurring theme in a number of his plays. How often do we see children being used as pawns in warfare waged by adults? Sometimes children are abducted and even killed by one mate to spite the other. Sometimes an adult who has a vendetta against another adult may take his or her vengeance out on the child or children of the transgressor. This situation is what Shakespeare portrays in the following excerpt. He presents a compelling picture of an innocent boy pleading for his life, asking not to be punished for an act his father committed. The boy's Tutor also begs for the boy's life, arguing that the boy's death would be offensive not only to mankind but also to God. In other words, it is a sin to harm the Innocents, he contends. The three speakers are the Earl of Rutland (the young boy who begs for his life), Lord Clifford (who intends to kill the boy—Rutland), and Rutland's Tutor.

Ah, Clifford, Murder Not This Innocent Child

Tutor: Ah, Clifford, murder not this innocent child,
Lest thou be hated both of God and man!
....

Rutland: So looks the pent-up lion o'er the wretch
That trembles under his devouring paws,
And so he walks, insulting o'er his prey,
And so he comes, to rend his limbs asunder.
Ah, gentle Clifford, kill me with thy sword,
And not with such a cruel threatening look.
Sweet Clifford, hear me speak before I die.
I am too mean a subject for thy wrath.
Be thou revenged on men, and let me live.

Clifford: In vain thou speak'st, poor boy. My father's blood***
Hath stopped the passage where thy words should enter.

Rutland: Then let my father's blood open it again.
He is a man, and, Clifford, cope with him.
(3 *Henry VI* 1. 3. 8-24)

***NOTE:** Rutland's father has killed Clifford's father.

PARAPHRASE

Tutor: Oh, Clifford, please do not murder this innocent child, unless you want to be hated or despised by both God and mankind.
....

Rutland: You look at me the way a frustrated lion scrutinizes his unfortunate prey that shudders under his destructive paws. And so he walks triumphant over his victim. He then comes to tear his limbs apart. Oh, kind Clifford, kill me with your sword and not with such a cold, menacing look. Dear Clifford, let me speak before I die. I am too unimportant to be the victim of your anger or vendetta. Take your revenge on adult males, and spare my life.

Clifford: My poor boy, begging for your life is useless. My father's blood has clogged the passage in my ear where your words should enter.

Rutland Then let my father's blood open this passage up again. He is a man—he is an adult. Settle matters with him.

He Had Two Sons

1. Gent: He had two sons—if this be worth your hearing,
Mark it—the eldest of them at three years old,
I' the swathing clothes the other, from their nursery
Were stolen, and to this hour no guess in knowledge
Which way they went.

2. Gent: How long is this ago?

1. Gent: Some twenty years.
(*Cymbeline* 1. 1. 58-63)

***NOTE:** In this discourse, two gentlemen are discussing a tragic incident that is far too frequent in our contemporary world: children being kidnapped—gone without a trace—sometimes for over twenty years, sometimes forever.

PARAPHRASE

1. Gent: He had two sons. If you care to hear about this case, then listen.. The older of the two was three years old. The other was an infant in swaddling clothes. They were stolen from their nursery, and to this hour, there is no knowledge (no one can even guess) where they went.

2. Gent: How long ago did this take place?

1. Gent: Some twenty years ago.

***NOTE:** In this segment, I decided to focus only on physical child abuse.

COMMENTARY: What Is Child Abuse? To Spank or Not to Spank; That Is the Question

This topic is a highly controversial one, hotly discussed in America today. The questions that remain unanswered are these: Where does parental spanking cross the line and enter the realm of physical child abuse? Is parental spanking, regardless how mild, ever justifiable?

In the Caribbean, corporal punishment was indigenous to our culture. At least, it was so when I was growing up. Parents used the whip or strap, even slippers, prolificly at home. Teachers used leather straps of good size and length also prolificly in elementary schools, and believe it or not, in Salem, a senior member of the community (usually female) could whip children who were misbehaving on the streets and send them home, subdued and crying, without repercussion. Actually, some parents were grateful for the additional corrective hand. I guess it did indeed "take a village."

Wow! What a difference today! Back then, there were no law suits, no police knocking at doors to cart parents or teachers off to jail, no social workers with governmental authority to take children to foster homes. In Montserrat and Antigua, because of the size and juxtaposition of most houses, whipping was rarely a private affair. On any given day, the shrieks of a neighborhood child would pierce the air. All passersby would know and accept the fact that Mr. or Mrs. So and So was beating his or her son or daughter for some infraction—perhaps failure to arrive home on time from school, failure to do chores, or commission of some other offense.

Sometimes, the hapless child would bolt outside, across the yard, into the neighboring vegetation and not venture back into the house until nightfall when the parent had fallen asleep. In those cases, missing dinner was not a problem. Hunger pangs were more readily chosen over leather welts or bruises from a tamarind whip. Perhaps the island parents took their cue from the passage in the Bible that asserts: Whom the Lord loves He chastens or chastises. The Caribbean parents must have "loved" a lot because the "chastenings" or "whoopings" were meted out frequently, without apology.

My siblings and I were fortunate in that spankings were few at our home as well as at certain other homes, but at school, we were all subject to the same physical punishment the other children endured. Even now, I recall how often leather straps landed across the backs of children at Salem Government Elementary School in Montserrat, at New Winthorpes Government Elementary School in Antigua, at Ottos Government Elementary School also in Antigua, and at all of the other government elementary schools in both islands. These leather straps were usually approximately three feet long and two inches thick. Further, the history of the Caribbean islands documents that corporal punishment was practiced in all the islands—the Greater as well as the Lesser Antilles.

I remember the atmosphere at Salem School when I was about six or seven years old. Any child who misbehaved was whipped. Any child who did not understand or absorb the subject matter taught in a given lesson was whipped. Any child who did not speak up in class when asked a question was whipped. Each day, all children who were tardy were whipped. One particular headmaster, Mr. Howard, wielded his leather strap with relish. He made it clear that rain was no excuse to arrive late to school. Remember, we all had to walk to school from various distances in the village. I recall his famous line as his strap descended mercilessly on the backs of tardy students on a rainy day: "You should have run between the drops!" he often exclaimed.

At Salem School (as in the typical elementary school), all classes (grades) met in one large room, so from my miniature chair in grade one, I could see the activities in all the higher grades in the room. Each day, all day, I remember seeing the leather strap flying in all of the upper classes in that room, particularly in the highest (most advanced) class taught by Mr. Howard. I remember being deeply concerned about my older sisters and cousins who occupied those classes, and I often found myself harboring a reluctance to grow up. I was relatively safe in kindergarten and first grade, but even there the teacher's ruler kept us in line.

In the highest grades—sixth and seventh, Mr. Howard applied his leather strap liberally especially when he taught math. He would line up all members of his class in front of the blackboard. Each student was given the chalk and asked to go to the blackboard. For every wrong answer, the strap descended. Naturally, the students were terrified. Of course, the other teachers in that room (especially the males) often followed suit, and whippings were frequent in their classes also. What is amazing is that students were able to concentrate and learn in an environment that should have inhibited learning. However, wonder of wonders, many brilliant students emerged from those classrooms across the Caribbean.

I must include one additional note about Mr. Howard. He suffered from epilepsy. Imagine the spectacle in that open schoolroom on any given day, when we saw Mr. Howard crash to the floor, in convulsive fits, just as he was about to speak, to ring the bell, or to whip someone. At such times, we students would freeze collectively while the teachers ministered to him. And then slowly, individually, we would exhale, with one thought: that what we had just witnessed was karma or justified retribution.

Speaking of retribution, I cannot close this chapter without referring to one last incident that occurred at Salem

School. One day, one of the male teachers (Mr. Munson) had taken his class outside for a lesson under the trees. Mr. Munson enjoyed wielding the whip. As expected, his whip soon descended on the backs of some of the students for one reason or another. Suddenly, one boy (a teenager) had had enough. After he had received a few lashes, he grabbed the whip and wrestled it from Mr. Munson's hand. He then began to strike Mr. Munson with the whip just as fast and as furiously as Mr. Munson had wielded the whip previously. Mr. Munson staggered backwards, and in less then no time, he was lying on the ground.

Imagine the panic! Imagine the confusion! All school activities came to a screeching halt at that moment. Nothing like this had ever occurred before. I cannot recall what punishment was meted out to the student, but he was not expelled as many expected. Who knows, perhaps even the island education officers recognized karma when they saw it.

Even as I write, I realize that the approach to teaching practiced in the government elementary schools across the Caribbean (as described above) was physical child abuse and nothing less. Let's give this behavior its right name. What puzzles me—that is, my adult perception—is that the parents, the government, the church, the whole community was complicit in this incorrect approach to learning. They must have been, because no one protested. Surely, I believe they meant well. It was common knowledge that centuries ago, in grammar schools in England, boys were caned or flogged. Some of the best and brightest adults, like Shakespeare, were schooled in that English system. So this corporal punishment in schools was the norm (and perhaps may still be) in British territories.

However, even now, I find myself wondering if there might have been one or two students with learning disabilities being drilled and whipped right along with the other students in those elementary schoolrooms. We will never know. What's more, even students who are not mentally challenged absorb materials at varying speeds. It is unconscionable to whip the slower ones. Some who read this discourse might remark, What's the fuss, anyway! Look how well we all turned out! That's true, but the same results could have been achieved with a kinder, gentler approach.

Truthfully, the indisputable fact is that most of us who were schooled in the British islands (those that emphasized discipline) turned out all right. One might, therefore, conclude that the end does indeed justify the means. I disagree. Granted, I don't know of anyone among us who is manifestly, psychologically scarred. The fact is that many island children grew up to be respectful, well-mannered achievers, but a more humane form of punishment could have yielded the same results.

It is common knowledge that spanking is often discouraged in America. I am the first to admit that many American children are disciplined, courteous achievers, but we cannot turn a blind eye or a deaf ear to the ones who are not. I have watched a significant number of American television shows, documentaries, as well as many scenes in supermarkets and elsewhere. I am usually appalled, speechless, as I see children—young children—kicking and spitting at their parents. Many of them unabashedly yell four-letter words at their submissive, docile, accommodating parents, most of whom behave as if "Thou shalt not spank" is one of the Ten Commandments. Their children usually demand and get whatever they want. They say "no" to everything and everyone, as they embarrass their parents. When I watch this disgraceful behavior, I find myself asking, Where are the straps or paddles? We all know that "go to your room" is quite often little or no punishment, since many of these rooms almost equal Disney World in attractions. So wherein lies the punishment? What is the answer?

Actually, my humble response to the question, should a parent spank or not spank, is that no extreme is either good or acceptable. Physical child abuse cannot be condoned. By the same token, childhood thugs should not be allowed to wage war and intimidate their parents and the rest of society. There are many successful, admirable Americans—achievers all—who were spanked as children. A periodic slap or two on a child's buttocks to keep him or her in line is not physical abuse and is, infact, good parenting.

15. MERCY VERSUS REVENGE

INTRODUCTION

In Shakespeare's England (sixteenth/seventeenth century) as well as before and after, theft was punishable by death. A few years ago, in Miami, a business man rigged his store with an electrical device after it was robbed repeatedly. Shortly after, the burglar who had robbed this store several times was found dead in the store—electrocuted by the device.

We may ponder the question, Was the device a deterrent or an instrument of revenge or both? How many of us are believers in the idea, "an eye for an eye, a tooth for a tooth," or does "Turn the other cheek" better reflect our attitude towards transgressors? The revenge motif is one of the most enduring themes in world literature. Unfortunately, revenge for murder has a domino effect, with the potential to wipe out entire families, as one murder is committed to avenge another. Is revenge sweet, as many believe, or is it just a tragic phenomenon that perpetuates human misery?

The Shakespearean passage that immediately follows documents the long feud that existed centuries ago between the Houses of Lancaster and York (the War of the Roses) that extended from generation to generation. Lord Clifford's vendetta is against Richard Plantagenet, the Duke of York. Lord Clifford is merciless and ruthless. His actions demonstrate that revenge can be vile and all-consuming, engulfing even the innocents. The following passage is a continuation of the dialogue between Clifford and the twelve-year-old Earl of Rutland (the Duke of York's young son) who is proclaiming his innocence and begging abjectly for his life to be spared (See chapter 14). Clifford's answer to Rutland is unyielding hatred and an insatiable appetite for revenge. Many who witness the following scene would be moved to tears.

Had I Thy Brethren Here

Clifford:　　Had I thy brethren here, their lives and Thine
　　　　　　Were not revenge sufficient for me.
　　　　　　No, if I digged up thy forefathers' graves
　　　　　　And hung their rotten coffins up in chains,
　　　　　　It could not slake mine ire, nor ease my heart.
　　　　　　The sight of any of the House of York
　　　　　　Is as a fury to torment my soul,

| | And till I root out their accursed line
And leave not one alive, I live in Hell.
Therefore----   [Lifting his hand.] |
|-----------|---|

Rutland: Oh, let me pray before I take my death!
           To thee I pray. Sweet Clifford, pity me!

Clifford: Such pity as my rapier's point affords.

Rutland: I never did thee harm. Why wilt thou slay
           Me?

Clifford: Thy father hath.

Rutland: But 'twas ere I was born.
           Thou hast one son. For his sake pity me,
           Lest in revenge thereof, sith God is just,
           He be as miserably slain as I.
           Ah, let me live in prison all my days,
           And when I give occasion of offense,
           Then let me die, for now thou hast no cause.

Clifford: No cause!
           Thy father slew my father. Therefore, die.
                                   [Stabs him.]
           (*3 Henry VI* 1. 3. 24-47)

PARAPHRASE

Clifford: If I had your brothers here, killing them along
           with you would not give me adequate
           satisfaction. No, if I were to dig up the
           graves of your forefathers and hang their
           rotten coffins in chains, it would not
           eliminate my anger or ease the pain in my
           heart. Whenever I see any member of the

	House of York, a wrath arises deep within me and tortures even my soul. I will live in Hell until I decimate or wipe out their entire cursed family and don't leave even one alive. Therefore-------[lifting his hand]
Rutland:	Oh, give me a chance to pray before I die! I am praying to you, Sweet Clifford. Have mercy on me.
Clifford:	The mercy that is found at the point of my sword.
Rutland:	I never hurt or offended you. Why do you want to kill me?
Clifford:	Your father has.
Rutland:	But the offense took place before I was born. You have one son. For his sake, have mercy on me, and since God is just, prevent him from being killed in revenge, as mercilessly as I. Oh, please let me live my entire life in prison, and when I offend you, only then you should kill me. But at this time, you have no cause to take my life.
Clifford:	No cause! Your father killed my father. Therefore, die. [stabs him]

*****NOTE:** In the following passage, what a stark contrast is seen in the foregoing view of ugly revenge and the sweet, Godly profile of mercy presented in one of Shakespeare's most famous passages. "To forgive" truly is "divine," he is saying in powerful, eloquent language.

The Quality of Mercy Is Not Strained

The quality of mercy is not strained,
It droppeth as the gentle rain from
Heaven
Upon the place beneath. It is twice blest;
It blesseth him that gives and him that takes.
'Tis mightiest in the mightiest. It becomes
The throned monarch better than his crown.
His scepter shows the force of temporal power,
The attribute to awe and majesty
Wherein doth sit the dread and fear of kings.
But mercy is above this sceptered sway,
It is enthroned in the hearts of kings,
It is an attribute to God himself,
And earthly power doth then show likest God's
When mercy seasons justice. Therefore, Jew,
Though justice be thy plea, consider this,
That in the course of justice none of us
Should see salvation. We do pray for mercy,
And that same prayer doth teach us all to render
The deeds of mercy.
(The Merchant of Venice 4.1. 184-202)

PARAPHRASE

Mercy in its purest form is not forced. (i.e., Mercy should be given spontaneously and freely.) It falls like mild rain from heaven to earth. It conveys a twofold blessing in that it blesses the one who gives it equally as it does the one who receives it. Mercy is mightiest (most impressive) when shown by the most powerful people. It adorns (or distinguishes) the monarch on his throne better than his crown does. A king's scepter signifies the power of his position which is characterized by awe and majesty and which evokes fear in others. But mercy towers above the power surrounding a monarch. (i.e., Possessing the ability to be merciful is more important than possessing the power or prestige of a king or queen.) Mercy is deeply rooted in the hearts of kings. It is an attribute or characteristic of God Himself; therefore, mortal power resembles God's when powerful rulers temper (i.e., soften) their laws by exercising mercy wherever necessary. Therefore, Jew, although you are demanding justice, consider the fact that if God were to abide strictly by the laws of justice, none of us would see salvation. Because we usually pray for mercy, we must also learn to be merciful in dealing with others.

***NOTE:** In the passage that follows, we hear the searing, urgent cry for revenge that the Ghost of Hamlet's father utters. There is no room for mercy here. Or is there? Are his words, "Leave her to heaven" an indication that he desires some form of mitigation, or is he hoping that heaven's punishment would be more severe than any meted out by man? In these famous words spoken by the Ghost, Shakespeare reminds us that there are two schools of thought or two approaches in the quest for revenge: those who are satisfied only when they, themselves, effect revenge and those who prefer to wait or back off and let heaven strike for them. Here is the situation in *Hamlet:*

The Ghost of the King of Denmark (Hamlet senior) appears to his son Hamlet (Prince of Denmark) with the devastating news that he was murdered in his sleep by his own brother (Hamlet's uncle) who took his throne as well as his wife (Hamlet's mother). He charges his wife with infidelity and possibly complicity in his murder. And yet, he proposes two different courses of revenge for the offending pair. He commissions Hamlet to murder his uncle as swiftly as possible. However, as far as his wife is concerned, he prefers to have God mete out punishment to her. We are not sure which punishment—God's or man's—he perceives as the more severe. Or, perhaps his decision stems from the fact that he is unwilling to ask his son to kill his own mother.

Leave Her to Heaven

Let not the royal bed of Denmark be
A couch for luxury and damned incest.
But, howsoever thou pursuest this act,
Taint not thy mind, nor let thy soul contrive
Against thy mother aught. Leave her to Heaven
And to those thorns that in her bosom lodge
To prick and sting her.

PARAPHRASE

Don't allow Denmark's royal bed to become a couch for lust and damned incest. But whatever method you use to exact revenge, don't stain either your mind or your soul in any plots against your mother. Let Heaven deal with her! And let her conscience prick, sting, and torment her.

COMMENTARY: Mercy or Revenge? That Is the Question

Consider the following situation. Harry Smith is arrested for killing Rita Jones. Because of a technicality, the jury is unable to convict Harry and charge him, beyond a reasonable doubt, with murder; therefore, he is released. However, the Jones family knows that Harry killed Rita. They have information from two eye witnesses who were too scared to testify at Harry's trial. Moreover, Harry is bragging all over town that he got away with murder.

After a while, members of the Jones family ambush Harry and kill him. Is the action of the Jones family justified? Is there any sympathy for them? An eye witness to Harry's murder contacts the police, and Charles and Robert Jones, the grief-stricken perpetrators, are arrested, tried, and sentenced to the electric chair.

After some time, the death sentence is about to be carried out. The governor of the state is bombarded by letters—some asking him to exercise mercy and spare the Jones brothers, others encouraging him to uphold the law which stipulates that premeditated murder is punishable by death.

Surprisingly, Mrs. Smith (Harry's mother) is one of those advocating a light sentence or even release for the Jones brothers. Unlike the Cliffords of this world, she believes in extending mercy rather than revenge.

Are you a proponent of mercy? Granted, sometimes the offense is so grave, it seems that only vengeance can bring inner peace. Naturally, most of us would never resort to criminal acts of vengeance, but how many of us can say that we have never been tempted to engage in little acts of revenge or retaliation, when our rights are trampled? I can't. It is only through fervent prayer that we can acquire the grace and the strength to let go and embrace God's promise: "Vengeance is mine; I will repay."

16. ASSASSINATION

INTRODUCTION

Assassination is another ugly word in our lexicon. Among the excerpts that follow, there are two of Shakespeare's most famous passages: one a great piece of oratory by Mark Antony, the other a soul-searching soliloquy by Macbeth who ponders introspectively the heinousness of murdering the innocent King Duncan. When I was twelve years old in Form 2A at Antigua Girls' High School, my English teacher, Ms. Mary Warrell, had us read and act out a number of Shakespeare's plays. *Julius Caesar* and *Macbeth* were among the plays we read and performed. I enjoyed Shakespeare's language immensely, but I recall the sadness I felt as I envisioned that moment in history when those senators stabbed away at the defenseless Roman Emperor. I also wished that I were near as Macbeth battled indecision, so that I could have whispered in his ear, "Don't do it! Don't kill the gracious King Duncan!"

I remember being most angry with Brutus for betraying Caesar who regarded him as his BFF—his best friend forever. Little wonder that as Mark Antony looks at Caesar's punctured body, he refers to the wound made by Brutus' dagger as the "most unkindest cut of all," and earlier, the dying Caesar asked the disturbing, guilt-provoking question, "Et tu Brute?" (You too, Brutus?)

In the passage that follows immediately, Brutus (who was a man of noble character) is trying in vain to justify his actions. Before Antony speaks, Brutus seeks to explain why he felt compelled to join the other senators in the murderous conspiracy against Caesar.

Romans, Countrymen, and Lovers!

Brutus: Romans, countrymen, and lovers! Hear me for my cause, and be silent, that you may hear. Believe me for mine honor, and have respect to mine honor, that you may believe. Censure me in your wisdom, and awake your senses, that you may the better judge. If there be any in this assembly, any dear friend of Caesar's, to him I say that Brutus' love to Caesar was no less than his. If then that friend demand why Brutus rose against Caesar, this is my answer—not that I loved Caesar less, but that I loved Rome more. Had you rather Caesar were living, and die all slaves, than that Caesar were dead, to live all freemen? As Caesar loved me, I weep for him; as he was fortunate, I rejoice at it; as he was valiant, I honor him. But as he was ambitious, I slew him. There is tears for

A Caribbean Accent to Shakespeare's Voice

	his love, joy for his fortune, honor for his valor, and death for his ambition. Who is here so base that would be a bondman? If any, speak, for him have I offended. Who is here so rude that would not be a Roman? If any, speak, for him have I offended. Who is here so vile that will not love his country? If any, speak, for him have I offended. I pause for a reply
All:	None, Brutus, none.
Brutus:	Then none have I offended. I have done no more to Caesar than you shall do to Brutus. The question of his death is enrolled in the Capitol, his glory not extenuated, wherein he was worthy, nor his offenses enforced, for which he suffered death. .... With this I depart—that, as I slew my best lover for the good of Rome, I have the same dagger for myself when it shall please my country to need my death. (*Julius Caesar* 3. 2. 13-43; 48-52)

PARAPHRASE

Brutus:	Beloved Romans, my countrymen! Give me the opportunity to defend or justify my actions. Please be quiet and listen. Trust my sense of fair play, and respect my ability to distinguish between right and wrong, so that you may have faith in my judgment. Exercise wisdom and discretion as you judge me, and be alert that you may be able to draw your conclusions more easily. If there is any

one of Caesar's close friends in this assembly, let me assure him that my love for Caesar was no less than his. If, therefore, that friend were to ask why I rose up against Caesar, here is my answer: It is not that I didn't love Caesar; it is rather that I love Rome far more. Would you have preferred Caesar were alive and you were all destined to die as slaves, or have him dead so that you can all live as free men? Because Caesar loved me, I weep for him; because he was successful, I rejoice; because he was valiant, I honor him. But because he was ambitious (despotic, power hungry), I killed him. There are tears for his love, joy for his success, honor for his valor, and death for his ambition. Who among you is so low in self-esteem that you would choose to be a slave? If there is anyone who fits this description, let him speak up, because I have offended him. Who among you is so low as not to feel pride in being a Roman? If there is one such person, let him speak, for he is the one I have offended. I pause for a reply.

All: None, Brutus, none.

Brutus: Then I have not offended anyone. I have done no more to Caesar than you shall do to me. The circumstance surrounding his death is preserved among the records in the Capitol. All his glory and all that made him praiseworthy is not in any way diminished, nor are his offenses that caused his death emphasized.

....

> Having said all I intended to say, I end my discourse with this final word: I executed a man, who loved me more than any other (and whom I loved more than any other), for the good of Rome. However, I have the same dagger to end my life whenever my country decides that it is necessary for me to die.

*****NOTE:** One of the most famous, best liked, and most often quoted passages from Shakespeare follows. Almost everyone knows the first sentence in this passage, just as most people know the first sentence of Hamlet's "To Be or Not To Be" soliloquy. Mark Antony is considered one of the greatest orators in history. He uses sarcasm (saying the opposite to what he really means) in order to sway the Roman people. For example, "honorable" becomes a dirty word as Antony hurls it repeatedly at Brutus and the other senators. His words are so well crafted that in less than no time, Caesar's accusers are profiled as villains and covetous murderers, while Caesar emerges as a hero in spite of the argument Brutus presented earlier. In reference to Brutus, whom he calls "Caesar's angel," Antony paints a most graphic, disturbing picture of betrayal. Let's not forget that Antony had to choose his words carefully and avoid arousing the ire of the conspirators who might have pounced on him and dispatched him as they had done Caesar. But, at first, Antony brilliantly and effectively cloaks his censure and condemnation in seemingly conciliatory words which help him to achieve his goal: to stir up the wrath of the Roman citizens against the senators who killed Julius Caesar simply because they were jealous of his greatness.

Friends, Romans, Countrymen, Lend Me Your Ears

Antony: Friends, Romans, countrymen, lend me your ears.
I come to bury Caesar, not to praise him.
The evil that men do lives after them;
The good is oft interred with their bones.
So let it be with Caesar. The noble Brutus
Hath told you Caesar was ambitious.
If it were so, it was a grievous fault,
And grievously hath Caesar answered it.
Here, under leave of Brutus and the rest—
For Brutus is an honorable man,
So are they all, all honorable men—
Come I to speak in Caesar's funeral.
He was my friend, faithful and just to me.
But Brutus says he was ambitious,
And Brutus is an honorable man.
He hath brought many captives home to Rome,
Whose ransoms did the general coffers fill.
Did this in Caesar seem ambitious?
When that the poor have cried, Caesar hath wept—
Ambition should be made of sterner stuff.
Yet Brutus says he was ambitious,
And Brutus is an honorable man.
You all did see that on the Lupercal
I thrice presented him a kingly crown,
Which he did thrice refuse. Was this ambition?
Yet Brutus says he was ambitious,
And, sure, he is an honorable man.
I speak not to disprove what Brutus spoke,
But here I am to speak what I do know.

	You all did love him once, not without cause. What cause withholds you then to mourn for him? O judgment, thou art fled to brutish beasts, And men have lost their reason! Bear with me, My heart is in the coffin there with Caesar, And I must pause till it come back to me.
1. Citizen: 2. Citizen:	Methinks there is much reason in his sayings. If thou consider rightly of the matter, Caesar has had great wrong.
3. Citizen:	Has he, masters? I fear there will a worse come in his place.
4. Citizen:	Marked ye his words? He would not take the crown. Therefore 'tis certain he was not ambitious.
1. Citizen:	If it be found so, some will dear abide it.
2. Citizen:	Poor soul! His eyes are red as fire with weeping.
3. Citizen:	There's not a nobler man in Rome than Antony.
4. Citizen:	Now mark him, he begins again to speak.
Antony:	But yesterday the word of Caesar might Have stood against the world. Now lies he There, And none so poor to do him reverence. O masters, if I were disposed to stir Your hearts and minds to mutiny and rage,

> I should do Brutus wrong and Cassius wrong
> Who, you all know, are honorable men.
> I will not do them wrong; I rather choose
> To wrong the dead, to wrong myself and you,
> Than I will wrong such honorable men.
> But here's a parchment with the seal of Caesar—
> I found it in his closet—'tis his will.
> Let but the commons hear this testament—
> Which, pardon me, I do not mean to read—
> And they would go and kiss dead Caesar's wounds
> And dip their napkins in his sacred blood,
> Yea, beg a hair of him for memory,
> And, dying, mention it within their wills,
> Bequeathing it as a rich legacy
> Unto their issue.

4. Citizen: We'll hear the will. Read it, Mark Antony.

All: The will, the will! We will hear Caesar's will.

Antony: Have patience, gentle friends. I must not read it.
It is not meet you know how Caesar loved you.
You are not wood, you are not stones, but men;
And, being men, hearing the will of Caesar,
It will inflame you, it will make you mad.
'Tis good you know not that you are his heirs,
For if you should, oh, what would come of it!

4. Citizen: Read the will. We'll hear it, Antony.
You shall read us the will, Caesar's will.

Antony:	Will you be patient? Will you stay awhile?
I have o'ershot myself to tell you of it.
I fear I wrong the honorable men
Whose daggers have stabbed Caesar. I do fear it.
4. Citizen:	They were traitors—honorable men!
All:	The will! The testament!
2. Citizen:	They were villains, murderers. The will! Read the will.
Antony:	You will compel me then to read the will?
Then make a ring about the corpse of Caesar,
And let me show you him that made the will.
Shall I descend? And will you give me leave?
....

If you have tears, prepare to shed them now.
You all do know this mantle. I remember
The first time ever Caesar put it on.
'Twas on a summer's evening, in his tent,
That day he overcame the Nervii.
Look, in this place ran Cassius' dagger through.
See what a rent the envious Casca made.
Through this the well-belovèd Brutus stabbed,
And as he plucked his cursèd steel away,
Mark how the blood of Caesar followed it,
As rushing out of doors, to be resolved
If Brutus so unkindly knocked, or no.
For Brutus, as you know, was Caesar's angel.
Judge, O you gods, how dearly Caesar loved him!
This was the most unkindest cut of all, |

> For when the noble Caesar saw him stab,
> Ingratitude, more strong than traitors' arms,
> Quite vanquished him. Then burst his mighty heart,
> And, in his mantle muffling up his face,
> Even at the base of Pompey's statue,
> Which all the while ran blood, great Caesar fell.
> Oh, what a fall was there, my countrymen!
> Then I, and you, and all of us fell down,
> Whilst bloody treason flourished over us.
> Oh, now you weep, and I perceive you feel
> The dint of pity. These are gracious drops.
> Kind souls, what weep you when you but behold
> Our Caesar's vesture wounded? Look you here—
> Here is himself, marred, as you see, with traitors.

1. Citizen: Oh, piteous spectacle!

2. Citizen: Oh, noble Caesar!

3. Citizen: Oh, woeful day!

4. Citizen: Oh, traitors, villains!

1. Citizen: Oh, most bloody sight!

2. Citizen: We will be revenged.

All: Revenge! About! Seek! Burn! Fire! Kill! Slay!
Let not a traitor live!

....

Antony: Good friends, sweet friends, let me not stir you up
To such a sudden flood of mutiny.
They that have done this deed are honorable.
What private griefs they have, alas, I know not,
That made them do it. They are wise and honorable,
And will, no doubt, with reasons answer you.
I come not, friends, to steal away your hearts.
I am no orator, as Brutus is,
But, as you know me all, a plain blunt man
That love my friend; and that they know full Well
That gave me public leave to speak of him.
For I have neither wit, nor words, nor worth,
Action, nor utterance, nor the power of speech,
To stir men's blood. I only speak right on,
I tell you that which you yourselves do know,
Show you sweet Caesar's wounds, poor poor Dumb mouths,
And bid them speak for me. But were I Brutus,
And Brutus Antony, there were an Antony
Would ruffle up your spirits, and put a tongue
In every wound of Caesar that should move
The stones of Rome to rise and mutiny.

All: We'll mutiny.

....

Antony: Why, friends, you go to do you know not what.

	Wherein hath Caesar thus deserved your loves? Alas, you know not. I must tell you, then— You have forgot the will I told you of.
All:	Most true, the will! Let's stay and hear the Will.
Antony:	Here is the will, and under Caesar's seal. To every Roman citizen he gives, To every several man, seventy-five drachmas.
2. Citizen:	Most noble Caesar! We'll revenge his death.
3. Citizen:	Oh, royal Caesar!
Antony:	Hear me with patience.
All:	Peace, ho!
Antony:	Moreover, he hath left you all his walks, His private arbors and new-planted orchards, On this side Tiber. He hath left them you, And to your heirs forever—common pleasures, To walk abroad and recreate yourselves. Here was a Caesar! When comes such another?
1. Citizen:	Never, never. Come, away, away! We'll burn his body in the holy place, And with the brands fire the traitors' houses. Take up the body.
2. Citizen:	Go fetch fire.

3. Citizen:	Pluck down benches.
4. Citizen:	Pluck down forms, windows, any thing. [Exeunt citizens with the body.]
Antony:	Now let it work. Mischief, thou art afoot, Take thou what course thou wilt. (*Julius Caesar* 3. 2. 78-164; 173-209; 214-235; 240-266)

PARAPHRASE

Antony:	My friends, my fellow Romans, my fellow citizens, please let me have your attention. I am here to bury Caesar, not to praise or honor him. The memory of the evil deeds that men commit often lingers long after their death, while their good deeds are often buried with them—forgotten. Let this be the case with Caesar. The noble Brutus has told you that Caesar was ambitious; if this was true, it was a very serious flaw in his nature, and he has borne the ultimate punishment for this flaw. Now, with the permission of Brutus and the others (Brutus is an honorable or respectable man; they are all honorable men); I have come to speak at Caesar's funeral. He was my friend; he was loyal and fair to men. But Brutus says Caesar was ambitious and Brutus is an honorable man. Caesar brought many prisoners of war home to Rome, and Rome profited from the ransom which boosted the revenue tremendously. Did this demonstrate ambition in Caesar? When the poor cried, Caesar cried with them. Ambition should be tougher than that. Yet Brutus

insists that Caesar was ambitious and Brutus is a respectable man. All of you can recall that on the Lupercal (a festival) three times I offered the crown to Caesar—three times I attempted to make him king—but each time, he refused the crown. Can you call his behavior ambition? Yet Brutus said he was ambitious (power hungry), and surely Brutus is a respectable man. I am not trying to contradict what Brutus said, but I am here to tell you what I know. All of you once loved Caesar, and you had good reason to do so. What is preventing you now from mourning for him? Good judgment has deserted men and entered wild beasts, and mankind has lost all rational powers! Have patience with me; my heart is in the coffin with Caesar, and I must pause until it comes back to me (until I regain my composure).

1.Citizen: I think that what he is saying makes a lot of sense.

2. Citizen: If you look at the situation carefully (fairly), Caesar has been seriously wronged.

3. Citizen: Has he? Is that true? Then I'm afraid that a worse ruler will replace him.

4. Citizen: Did you hear Antony's words? He would not take the crown. Therefore, surely, he was not ambitious.

1. Citizen: If this turns out to be the case, someone (some people) will pay dearly for it (Caesar's death).

2. Citizen:	Poor soul! His eyes are red as fire with weeping.
3. Citizen:	There's not a nobler man in Rome than Antony.
4. Citizen:	Now listen to him; he is beginning to speak once more.
Antony:	Only yesterday Caesar may have commanded the world. Now he lies there with not even the poorest, most insignificant man to honor him. Gentlemen! If I were inclined to stir up anger and rebellion within you, I would be doing an injustice to Brutus and Cassius who, you all know, are honorable men. I will not offend them. I prefer to offend the dead, to offend myself, and you, before I displease such honorable men. But here's a sheet of paper with Caesar's seal. I found it in his closet. It is his will. If only the masses were to hear this will (testament)—which, excuse me, I do not intend to read—they would kiss the wounds on Caesar's corpse and dip their handkerchiefs in his sacred blood or seek to procure a strand of his hair as a souvenir, and on their death beds they would include it in their wills as a prized possession---an heirloom—to be passed on to their children.
4. Citizen:	We want to hear the will. Read it, Mark Antony.
All:	The will, the will! Let us hear Caesar's will.
Antony:	Be patient, kind friends. I should not read it.

	It is not advisable for you to know how much Caesar loved you. You are not inanimate wood or stones but human. And because you are human, hearing the will of Caesar will inflame you, will stir up anger within you. It is good that you do not know that you are Caesar's heirs, for if you should know, consider the consequence!
4. Citizen:	Read the will. We want to hear it, Antony. Read Caesar's will to us.
Antony:	Will you be patient? Will you wait a while? I have gone ahead of myself to tell you about it. I am afraid that I wrong the honorable men whose daggers have stabbed Caesar. I believe I have.
4. Citizen:	They were traitors! Honorable men, ha!
All:	The will! The testament!
2. Citizen:	They were villains, murderers. The will! Read the will.
Antony:	Will you compel me then to read the will? Then form a circle around Caesar's body, and let me show you the man who wrote the will. May I descend? And will you give me permission?
	………………………………………………..
	If you are capable of crying, get ready to weep now. You know this cloak. I remember the first time Caesar wore it. It was an evening in the summer, in his tent.

That day he had conquered the Nervii (people Caesar defeated as he amassed territory for Rome). Look! Cassius's dagger pierced this hole. Notice what a slit the envious Casca made. Through this hole, Caesar's favorite—Brutus—stabbed; and as he withdrew his cursed (damned, wretched) sword, notice how Caesar's blood followed it, as if it rushed outside to determine whether Brutus had struck so cruelly, for as you know, Brutus was Caesar's angel. Judge, you gods, how dearly Caesar loved him. This was the most cruel cut of all, for when noble Caesar saw Brutus stab him, Ingratitude which is more powerful than the arms of traitors overpowered him, and his mighty heart gave way. (In other words, Caesar died from a broken heart at Brutus's ingratitude and treachery rather than from the wounds made by the swords.) With his cloak covering his face, great Caesar died at the foot of Pompey's statue from which blood flowed. My countrymen! What a tremendous (resounding) fall that was. When Caesar fell, you and I and all of us fell too, while bloody treason flourished over us. O, now you weep, and I notice that you feel the stroke of pity. You shed compassionate tears. Kind souls, do you weep after merely seeing Caesar's sword-pierced cloak? Look, here is Caesar's body mutilated by traitors.

1. Citizen: Oh, pitiful sight!

2. Citizen: Oh, noble Caesar!

3. Citizen:	Oh, woeful day!
4. Citizen:	Oh, traitors, villains!
1. Citizen:	Oh, most bloody sight!
2. Citizen:	We will seek vengeance.
All:	Revenge! About! Seek! Burn! Fire! Kill! Slay! We won't allow even one traitor to live!
Antony:	Good friends, kind friends, don't let me stir you up or provoke you to such sudden rebellion. The men who have executed Caesar are honorable. I don't know what individual grievances they have had against Caesar to have made them assassinate him. They are wise and honorable, and they will, undoubtedly, give you reasons for their action. I am not here, friends, to gain your favor. I am not a speaker of Brutus's caliber. Instead, I am a plain, blunt (honest) man who loves my friend; this fact they know very well. That's why they gave me permission to speak in public about Caesar. However, I am neither witty nor eloquent nor important; neither have I distinguished myself in action. I only speak honestly to an issue, telling you what you already know. I am here to show you sweet Caesar's wounds which appear to be poor, silent mouths. These mouths I ask to speak for me. However, if I were Brutus and Brutus were Antony, Antony would stir you with indignation putting a tongue in each of

	Caesar's wounds, giving it the power to move the stones in the streets of Rome and persuade them to rise up and rebel and avenge Caesar's death.
All:	We'll mutiny.
1. Citizen:	We'll burn Brutus's house.
3. Citizen:	Let's go then. Come! Let us go find the conspirators.
Antony:	Wait! Listen to me, my countrymen, let me speak.
All:	Be quiet everyone. Let's listen to Antony, most noble Antony!
Antony:	My friends, you are about to leave without adequate information. What reason do you have for loving Caesar so much? Sadly, you don't know. Therefore, I must tell you. You have forgotten the will I mentioned earlier.
All:	That's true, the will! Let's stay and hear the will.
Antony:	Here's the will, and it is sealed by Caesar. To every Roman citizen—to every individual man—he gives seventy-five drachmas.
2. Citizen:	Most noble Caesar! We'll revenge his death.
3. Citizen:	Oh, royal Caesar!
Antony:	Be patient and listen to me.

All:	Be quiet!
Antony:	What's more, Caesar has left all of his private grounds, his arbors, and newly-planted orchards on this side of the Tiber (a river flowing through Rome). He has left all of this to you and your children forever. He has left all of this land for the general public, for your recreation, for you to walk about and enjoy yourselves. Here was a Caesar! When will there ever be another like Him?
1. Citizen:	Never, never. Let's go! We'll burn his body in the holy place, and then with the torches, we will set fire to the traitors' houses. Lift up the body.
2. Citizen:	Go get fire.
3, Citizen:	Tear down benches.
4. Citizen:	Tear down buildings, windows, anything.
Antony:	Now, let vengeance take over. Revenge, take charge; get ready to act. Take whatever course of action you see fit.

A soliloquy is a monologue—a character speaks to himself or herself while the audience overhears the speech and often witnesses the character's psychological conflict, even inner turmoil. The following is one of the most famous soliloquies among Shakespeare's works and in all English literature. Like Hamlet's "To be or not to be" soliloquy, it is immortal and demonstrates the agony of making moral decisions that would yield dire consequences in this life and the afterlife. As we listen, we hear Macbeth struggling with the idea of assassinating the innocent King Duncan. He is unable to find even one justifiable reason for killing the kind king. Consequently, from this oyster-like friction of good and evil, emerges a deathless gem—an image of Pity or Goodness in its purest form, housed in the body of quintessential innocence: "a naked newborn babe," as Shakespeare puts it. What a great representation to be used by any speaker or writer who seeks to portray, in compelling language, the stark difference between good and evil!

If It Were Done When 'Tis Done

If it were done when 'tis done, then 'twere
Well
It were done quickly. If the assassination
Could trammel up the consequence, and catch,
With his surcease, success, that but this blow
Might be the be-all and the end-all here,
But here, upon this bank and shoal of time,
We'd jump the life to come. But in these cases
We still have judgment here, that we but teach
Bloody instructions, which being taught return
To plague the inventor. This even-handed justice
Commends the ingredients of our poisoned chalice
To our own lips. He's here in double trust.
First, as I am his kinsman and his subject,
Strong both against the deed. Then, as his host,
Who should against his murderer shut the door,
Not bear the knife myself. Besides, this Duncan

Hath borne his faculties so meek, hath been
So clear in his great office, that his virtues
Will plead like angels trumpet-tongued against
The deep damnation of his taking-off.
And pity, like a naked newborn babe,
Striding the blast, or Heaven's cherubin horsed
Upon the sightless couriers of the air,
Shall blow the horrid deed in every eye,
That tears shall drown the wind. I have no spur
To prick the sides of my intent, but only
Vaulting ambition, which o'erleaps itself
And falls on the other.
(*Macbeth* 1. 7. 1-28)

PARAPHRASE

If the act of murder could only end when the blow is struck, then it would be all right to do it quickly. If the murder could have no negative consequences but could be final and successful at Duncan's death! If only this blow could help me achieve my goal without any repercussions! If this were possible in this life, then the afterlife would be no risk. However, unfortunately, in cases like murder, we must always face retribution here on this earth, and when we do bloody or violent deeds, deeds equally violent are often done to us. Impartial justice usually makes us drink the poison we prepared for someone else. He (Duncan) is here, in good faith, for two reasons: first, because I am his relative and his subject—these are two strong links to Duncan that should discourage me from assassinating him. In addition, as his host, I should be the one to shut the door to protect him from a potential murderer, not murder him myself. Besides, Duncan has conducted himself so well in his high position as king; he has remained so meek, so unassuming, in spite of the great power of his office; he has been so innocent, so virtuous, that his virtues will cry out like angels with voices like trumpets, outraged at the damnable, heinous murder of the king. And pity in the form of a naked, newborn baby carried by the wind, or a cherubim riding on the unseen messengers of the air, will blow the terrible deed in every eye, that the volume of tears would be sufficient to drown the wind. I have nothing to spur me on to commit the deed and make my dream a reality except an unstable ambition which flairs up and subsides at intervals.

I Have Given Suck

I have given suck, and know
How tender 'tis to love the babe that milks me.
I would, while it was smiling in my face,
Have plucked my nipple from his boneless gums
And dashed the brains out, had I so sworn as you
Have done to this.
(*Macbeth* 1. 7. 54-58)

*****NOTE:** Lady Macbeth is speaking in the above passage. She is one of the most notorious she-devils in literature. As her words indicate, she is cold and heartless. She goads her husband on to kill Duncan, providing the "spur" that would "prick the sides of [his] intent," proving to be even more ruthless than he.

PARAPHRASE

I have suckled an infant, and therefore I have experienced the tender love that flows from a mother to the baby at her breast. However, even while my baby was smiling up at me, I would have snatched my nipple from his or her toothless gums and I would have shattered his brains if I had previously sworn to do so, as you have sworn to kill Duncan.

Delpha Charles, Ph.D.

COMMENTARY: The Plurality of Assassination

As demonstrated in the above passage from *Julius Caesar*, when a leading public figure is murdered, we the people become embroiled in the emotional maelstrom of assassination—its plurality—as I have labeled it. Let me elaborate. I believe that even the Roman children must have been affected by the riotous warfare that ensued in the wake of Caesar's assassination. It was October 45 B.C. Not long before his death, Julius Caesar—the greatest Roman Emperor of all—had recently returned to Rome after twelve years of victories in countries such as Gaul, Spain, Egypt, Africa, and Asia Minor where the Roman culture had a beneficial impact. He had practically conquered the ancient world and had returned to Rome to clean up the corruption in the Roman Republic. Naturally, the power- hungry and corrupt aristocrats and leaders felt threatened at Caesar's return, but the people of Rome were ecstatic as they welcomed their hero—Caesar—home.

Picture the adoring multitude that lined the streets to greet the victorious general who entered the city with government officials as well as his vast army and many prisoners. Imagine the jubilation, the myriad hands clapping, the shouts of adoration, the bells, the trumpets, free food and drinks for all. A comparable scene was evidenced in 1660 England at the Restoration of Charles II to the British throne. With a collective roar (not sigh) of relief, millions lined the streets of London not only to welcome and escort their returning king to the throne but also to celebrate the end of Puritan rule under Oliver Cromwell.

Other similar scenes of celebration are our modern-day ticker tape parades like the one down Fifth Avenue in honor of the astronauts—Neil Armstrong, Edwin ("Buzz") Aldrin, Jr., and Michael Collins. Armstrong and Aldrin were the first humans to walk on the moon on July 21, 1969. Their Lunar Module—the Eagle—spent twenty-one hours, thirty-one minutes on the lunar surface, while Collins remained in orbit in the Command Module—the Columbia. The three astronauts returned to earth on July 24 and, like Caesar, were greeted by a massive, exuberant crowd.

I can imagine the joyful shrieks of the Roman children on the day of Caesar's return. They, too, must have tried hard to catch a glimpse of this important man whom they had never seen before. How could they have known that for this great hero, the Ides of March would have come inexorably, the soothsayer's warning notwithstanding? How could they have known that they as well as their parents would have been affected by the assassination of their Emperor? None of those children had ever heard the word "assassination." It is not of Latin origin. It entered the English language many centuries later. However, perhaps for the first time, their innocent world was violated by the murder of a beloved leader.

The first time I ever encountered the word "assassin," I was a child approximately six or seven years old in the island of Montserrat. When I read of the misadventures of Pinocchio, I desperately wanted him to get back home safely to Gezeppo each time he ventured out, and I was sad and frustrated each time something occurred that interfered with the likelihood of his becoming a real boy. Sadly, I read that as he walked home one day, "he fell among assassins." Those are the exact words I read. My first reaction was to find out from my mother what was an "assassin," and then I cried for poor Pinocchio. Why did the assassins have to hurt him, I asked myself. All he ever wanted was to be safe and become a real boy.

Through this experience, I learned early that this world could be an unfriendly place with assassins running around, hurting innocent people, even children. Later, I discovered the plurality of assassination: The victims are legion when a good leader is struck down.

I remember sitting with my ears glued to the radio (we had no television then), in the island of Antigua, the day President John F. Kennedy was buried. It was not just America that mourned; the island of Antigua mourned right along with America that day. In fact, the world seemed to have stood still in bereavement that day. Even the animals seemed to have sensed that something was amiss.

As the funeral cortege made its way to Arlington Cemetery, each clap, clap, clap of the horses' hooves evoked tears while the world said goodbye to a great leader. The assassination of his brother (Robert Kennedy) and Martin Luther King, Jr. a few years later was equally agonizing. Once more, I found myself a weeping victim of assassination. How can we ever adequately express our gratitude for the societal changes which these brave men paid the ultimate price to effect? Julius Caesar was killed before Christ was born, and Abraham Lincoln was murdered in 1865 after he had taken the first unparalleled steps to enforce the God-given, "unalienable Rights" of black Americans, as stated in the Declaration of Independence. It must be noted here that those who mourned the passing of these great men far outnumber those who hated them, for even now as history is told and retold, written and rewritten, we find ourselves touched by the pathos surrounding their senseless killing. In such instances, we are indeed caught up in what I term the plurality of assassination.

A Caribbean Accent to Shakespeare's Voice

17. FATNESS/OBESITY

INTRODUCTION

The world of fashion and glamour often discriminates against fat people. Plus size garments are avoided like the plague, even by those who should be wearing them, and many people are starving, pummeling, suctioning, and brutalizing themselves in order to be thin. By stark contrast, in one of the passages that follow, through the voice of Caesar, Shakespeare expresses preference for people with a good measure of flesh on their bones. He says he feels more comfortable in their presence than in the company of people with a "lean and hungry" look. He insists that he trusts overweight men more readily than he does men who are thin.

When Shakespeare wrote approvingly of overweight people, it is quite possible that he was speaking from the heart and not merely facetiously allowing his characters to voice what he might or might not have believed. Look at how he portrays the kind, lovable, obese Falstaff, one of the mischievous companions of the young Prince Henry—Harry—(later King Henry V). In order to ready himself to become king, Prince Henry decided to put aside his reckless ways by distancing himself from Falstaff and the rest of his youthful companions. Here are the words Shakespeare has Falstaff say to the prince in an effort to persuade the prince to keep him as his friend:

If To Be Fat Be To Be Hated

If to be fat be to be hated, then Pharaoh's lean kine***
are to be loved. No, my good lord. Banish Peto,
banish Bardolph, banish Points. But for sweet Jack
Falstaff, kind Jack Falstaff, true Jack Falstaff, valiant
Jack Falstaff, and therefore more valiant, being, as he
is, old Jack Falstaff, banish not him thy Harry's company.
Banish plump Jack, and banish all the world.
(*I Henry IV* 2.4. 519-526)

***NOTE:** In the above passage, Shakespeare (through Falstaff) makes a Biblical allusion to Joseph's interpretation of Pharaoh's dream (*Genesis* 41: 1-45). This king of the great empire of Egypt was tremendously impressed with Joseph when he was able to reveal the meaning of the king's dream, while the so-called wise men in the kingdom could not. "Kine" is an archaic word for "cows." In his dream,

Pharaoh saw seven fat cows and seven lean (skinny) cows. Joseph explained that the seven fat cows signified seven good years of plenty that Egypt would enjoy, while the skinny cows represented seven tough years of famine that would follow. Naturally, Falstaff's argument is that fat is good and welcome, particularly in this context, since the lean cows were hungry predators which ate up all of the fat cows.

PARAPHRASE

If fatness is automatically shunned, even hated, then Pharaoh's skinny cows should be lovable. No, my good lord. Distance yourself from Peto, Bardolph, and Poins. But as far as Jack Falstaff is concerned—the sweet , kind, true, valiant Jack Falstaff—please don't desert him, seeing that he is even more valiant now that he is old. Please don't deprive him of your friendship. If you were to abandon your fat friend, you would lose your whole world.

***NOTE: In the following passage, Caesar is voicing his preference for fatness, declaring that he feels more safe, more comfortable around men who are fat. Ironically, Caesar had every reason to fear Cassius, not because he was thin but because he was Caesar's chief enemy, one of the main conspirators, actively planning Caesar's assassination. As if by premonition, the unwitting Caesar feels uncomfortable in his presence, even as Antony, unaware that Cassius is the primary instigator in Caesar's demise, makes the ironic statement: "He's not dangerous."

Let Me Have Men About Me That Are Fat

Caesar: Let me have men about me that are fat,
          Sleek-headed men, and such as sleep o'

nights.
Yond Cassius has a lean and hungry look.
He thinks too much, such men are dangerous.

Antony: Fear him not, Caesar. He's not dangerous.
He is a noble Roman, and well given.

Caesar: Would he were fatter! But I fear him not.
Yet if my name were liable to fear,
I do not know the man I should avoid
So soon as that spare Cassius.
(*Julius Caesar* I. 2. 192-201)

PARAPHRASE

Caesar: Let me be surrounded by fat, level-headed men who sleep at nights (i.e., instead of lying awake thinking and scheming). That man Cassius over there looks skinny and hungry. He thinks too much; such men are dangerous.

Antony: Don't be afraid of him, Caesar. He is not dangerous. He is a noble, well-disposed Roman.

Caesar: I wish he were fatter. But I am not afraid of him. However, if my name (i.e., my station, my rank) permitted me to be fearful—If I were inclined to be scared, I don't know any other person I would avoid as readily as that thin Cassius.

COMMENTARY: The Lean and Hungry Look

When I was growing up in the Caribbean, the lean and hungry look was not fashionable. Thinness was not all the craze as it is today. In fact, those days, especially in Montserrat, among the women who were considered attractive, even beautiful, were those who were said to be "fat and nice." "Rosey," "curvaceous," "plump," and "well covered" were all favorable descriptors, no euphemism intended. A summation of those words would be equivalent to our contemporary term, "sexy." Of course, as a teenager, I was dissatisfied with my weight. It was not by choice that I was a member of the group that Julius Caesar would have found unattractive were he a resident of Montserrat or Antigua when I was growing up. You see, I had the "lean and hungry look."

For quite some time, I made a concerted effort to gain weight by eating as much icecream as possible. Consuming the last scrap of food on my plate at every meal also became my modus vivendi—my way of life. However, all of my effort was to no avail. If I had lived in Rome during Caesar's time, I would have hoped that his preference for fatness applied only to men. As I struggled to gain weight, one day a friend of mine suggested that I take a substance called "weight-on." Imagine the irony! Today, I regret every tablespoon of weight-on I ingested back then.

Naturally, I was not alone in my effort to cast off the "lean and hungry look." The older sister of a friend of mine was determined to gain weight before her wedding day arrived. How ironic! Today, prospective brides torture themselves to lose even one pound. In any case, my friend's sister postponed the date of her wedding while she consumed bottle after bottle of weight-on. Unfortunately, she did not achieve the desired results, and during the time her fiancé waited, he decided to marry someone else.

Of course, since those days, many of us now recognize that what is important is to do whatever is necessary to maintain good health. We should all adopt the Latin motto: *mens sana in corpore sano*—a healthy mind in a healthy body.

18. DRESS/CLOTHES

INTRODUCTION

In his book entitled *Shakespeare's England: Life in Elizabethan & Jacobean Times,* R. E. Pritchard has recorded the words of a sixteenth-century eye witness who describes in detail the preoccupation with clothing and fashion in Shakespeare's world. In essence, Shakespeare's contemporary is denouncing the vanity of his peers and their obsession with clothes. He reveals that men and women alike cast aside all thought of expense in order to appear in the latest fashions. As soon as they wear one costly outfit, a day or two later, it is abandoned for another newly arrived from France or elsewhere. What fussing! What preening! What constant changing from head to toe! What sums of money wasted in clothing, he laments. He decries the fact that so much attention is given to the body, and not one wit to the soul. As I read, it was as if I were viewing our world of fashion in Hollywood, New York, Paris, and elsewhere.

How often do we see women on television talk shows confessing their addiction to shopping, revealing the numerous shoes and outfits they own, seeking help for their obsession with clothes. Some don't have enough money to pay their bills or even to buy adequate food. Some are facing foreclosure and are on the verge of declaring bankruptcy, yet they shop frequently with plastic "money," foolishly purchasing expensive designer fashions they can't afford. These are the type of people that Shakespeare labels and dismisses in the metaphor: nuts without "kernel," not to be trusted with weighty matters.

There Can Be No Kernel in This Light Nut

There can be no kernel in this light nut. The soul of this man is his clothes. Trust him not in matter of heavy consequence. *(All's Well That Ends Well* 2. 5. 47-49)

PARAPHRASE

There is no substance in this man. He may be compared to a nut with no kernel. This man is preoccupied with his clothes. Do not seek or expect any participation from him in serious matters.

Costly Thy Habit as Thy Purse Can Buy

Costly thy habit as thy purse can buy,
But not expressed in fancy—rich, not gaudy.
For the apparel oft proclaims the man.
(*Hamlet* 1. 3. 70-73)

***NOTE:** In the passage above, Polonius is giving Laertes, his son, timely advice in clothing and general deportment just before Laertes leaves for France. "The clothes make the man" is a famous expression made in essence here, possibly originating with Shakespeare.

PARAPHRASE

Let the cost of your clothing be commensurate with the money you possess. Don't wear outlandish clothes. Let your clothing be rich, not gaudy; for a man's (or woman's) clothes often proclaim to the world who he (or she) is.

Delpha Charles, Ph.D.

COMMENTARY: My Purple Shoes in Antigua—Pride and Unfortunate Consequences

During my adolescent years, I had an eye for fashion. I would always stare admiringly at the glamorous women whom I saw on the streets or at church and hope to be able to dress like them when I grew up. Even as I wore the ordinary, run-of-the-mill clothing, I always wished to have dresses and shoes that were pretty and different from the ordinary. Those days, in Antigua, any item of clothing that was original and specially designed most likely bore the "Made in America" tag.

One day, when I was approximately ten years old, Fortune was gracious to me. A package arrived for my family from my sister in New York. Among the items that bore my name was a special pair of shoes. I had never seen any shoes like those before. Ever heard of shocking pink? Well, these shoes were shocking purple. They were open at the back and enclosed at the toes, with sturdy two-inch heels. Now, in those days in the islands, shoes came in two or three basic, traditional colors: black, white, and brown with an occasional red or pink for ladies.

I rushed to try on my bright purple shoes with their attractive buckles in front. They were comfortable and quite stylish. That very afternoon, I had to go to the shopping center in the heart of St. John's town, and so naturally, I proudly set out in my new purple shoes which permitted me to feel stylish, finally. My mother sent me to a building on the most populous street—Market Street. It was (perhaps still is) a narrow street located in the center of the town, extending for a good distance from north to south. Cars were few in those days, so I was able to walk freely, leisurely, proudly without dodging traffic.

Suddenly, as I strutted down the street, I heard loud laughter. I turned my head to see a group of men and women walking close behind me and pointing to my shoes. They were carrying shovels and other tools that indicated that they were on their way home from work. Obviously, they were delighted to have any distraction to brighten the last lap of their dreary day. To my dismay, I discovered that I was the diversion. Their cackling, raucous laughter got louder by the minute, and the pointing and the taunts increased. "A whey you get dem shoes!" they shouted. Their broken English seemed to make the heckling more jolting: "Wha kinda shoes she a wear?" Soon other pedestrians in the vicinity joined this group, eager to participate in the amusement, at my expense.

Before long, these cruel, motley, sweaty, unkempt hecklers were walking relentlessly behind me, creating such a commotion that people in two-story houses on both sides of the street pushed their windows up and stuck their necks out to see what was the source of the uproar. To say that I was embarrassed is an understatement. My knees felt weak. I was trembling. I wanted to disappear into thin air, but I couldn't, so I simply kept moving forward in unsteady, unsure steps. Then, oh Mercy! Like a flash, my knees buckled, and I fell to the ground.

When I fell, the laughter soared to a rasping crescendo. In less than no time, I was on my feet again, unscathed physically but damaged emotionally. To this day, I don't remember how I escaped that trying encounter. And now as I recall the incident, I am wondering how adults could have been so cruel and insensitive to anyone but least of all to a child. I believe my readers are asking the same question. That day, even in childhood, I discovered that people are often intolerant of any person, idea, or thing that is strange or different from what is common place to them, even something as harmless as the color of a child's shoes. It is this intolerance that undergirds racial prejudice. Unfortunately, It is this intolerance that often triggers skirmishes and warfare and worldwide carnage. In jest, I must say that I also learned another lesson from that incident: that sometimes pride literally goes before a fall.

19. RACIAL PREJUDICE

INTRODUCTION

I did not know the meaning of racial prejudice until I came to America. In Montserrat and Antigua, we were all one race: African-Caribbean or AfroCaro (my coinage). And so, bright-eyed and amiable, I arrived in America fully prepared to love my neighbors (of all races) if not quite as myself, as close to that as possible. Unfortunately, I have since made an unwelcome acquaintance with racial prejudice—one of the oldest, most deadly, most insidious destroyers of mankind since planet earth was created and since mankind became aware and intolerant of fellow human kind.

It is not for me to rewrite history here. We are all cognizant of the fact that racial prejudice has spawned massacres, civil wars, holocausts, ethnic cleansing, and unspeakable crimes worldwide. Racial prejudice may be termed a social, incurable, visceral cancer whose cells multiply subliminally, and metastasize exponentially, only to surface and strike in various ways, in various places, even as a cure is sought in vain.

Shakespeare's world was not exempt from racism. The Jews were the primary victims. In Elizabethan England, anti-Semitism was rife and practiced as the norm. From since Biblical times, we learn that "the Jews had no dealing with Gentiles" and obviously vice versa. I can imagine that countless innocent Jewish and Gentile children were confused, wondering why they couldn't play with certain other children; that is, until they grew up and *learned* why. Notice my emphasis. Racism is not genetic. It is acquired by example and indoctrination.

Most people in Shakespearean England never encountered even one Jew. Actually, King Edward I (1239-1307) had expelled all Jews from England hundreds of years before Shakespeare's time. And yet the negative, stereotypical picture of Jews was kept alive in literature as well as in daily interaction with the Jews who returned and remained a small minority. Hatred of Jews was seminal. They were regarded as cruel, twisted, greedy, money-hungry, selfish unbelievers. They were blamed for all social ills including the Bubonic Plague and were persecuted mentally and physically. Not even the personal physician of Queen Elizabeth I could escape this inherent racial condemnation. Though her Jewish physician was baptized as a Christian, he was falsely accused of treason and was hanged, drawn, and quartered. It is said that the queen was deeply saddened at his loss but felt powerless to intervene and face the powerful tidal wave of anti-Semitism.

Naturally, the dramatists and other writers of the Elizabethan age presented their audiences exactly what they expected: the evil Jew creating daily havoc. For example, Christopher Marlowe (one of Shakespeare's contemporaries) wrote a play entitled *The Jew of Malta* in which Barabas, the cruel, avaricious protagonist, goes about poisoning wells and killing innocent people.

Shakespeare's Shylock in *The Merchant of Venice* is akin to Barabas. He is a hateful and spiteful Jew. As if to avenge, even symbolically, the racism directed at all Jews, Shylock demands a pound of flesh from the Christian—Antonio—who is unable to repay the loan of three thousand ducats. It is from Shakespeare that "a pound of flesh" has been incorporated into our parlance to represent an unreasonable, perhaps even deadly, demand one person may impose on another.

In Shakespearean literature, black people also emerge as victims of racism. In the fifteenth century, the Portuguese explored the coasts of west Africa and brought back black slaves to Europe. After a while, it was customary to call Africans "Moors." Blacks were often portrayed as villains, unsavory, not to be trusted. And so, in *The Merchant of Venice*, we hear the Prince of Morocco saying to Portia, "Mislike me not for my complexion...." Obviously, the dark color of his skin was reason enough for rejection. Moors are profiled negatively in a number of Shakespeare's plays perhaps because this portrayal is what the audience expected. For example, in *Titus Andronicus*, Aaron the Moor is a villain; he is Queen Tamora's secret lover.

The visceral prejudice against black people could hardly be demonstrated more effectively than it is in *Titus Andronicus*. When Tamora gives birth to a child fathered by Aaron, she considers her baby boy repulsive, loathsome, hideous, and comparable to a toad. She orders his death shortly after his birth. Her two adult sons also find the child detestable. They refuse to regard him as their brother, and they also announce that he is worthy of death.

Another example of negative racial profiling is seen in *Othello* where an interracial marriage in Venice ends badly. Desdemona is a Venetian lady, daughter of a senator and married to Othello the Moor. He is a noble Venetian statesman, and yet he commits a deplorable act of murder, strangling his defenseless wife while she lies in bed. This act may be construed as yet another instance of anti-Black stereotyping.

    Let me, therefore, reiterate the fact that as a child in the Caribbean, I saw racial prejudice only in the literature I read. I recall the days I innocently frolicked with my classmates on the grounds of the Antigua Girls' High School (AGHS) oblivious of the deadly impact of racism. We Caribbean school girls were as carefree as the Eton boys whom Thomas Gray (1716-1771) observed and wrote about in his "Ode on a Distant Prospect of Eton College," emphasizing their unawareness of future ills and stressing the need to keep them in blissful ignorance. The same lines could have been written about us, AGHS girls:

> Alas! Regardless of their doom
>   The little victims play;
> No sense have they of ills to come,
>   Nor care beyond today:
> Yet see, how all around 'em wait
> The ministers of human Fate,
>   And black Misfortune's baleful train!
> Ah, show them where in ambush stand,
> To seize their prey, the murth'rous band!
>   Ah, tell them they are men
> . . . .
>
> To each his suff'rings: all are men,
>   Condemn'd alike to groan;
> The tender for another's pain,
>   Th' unfeeling for his own.
> Yet, ah! Why should they know their
>   Fate?
> Since sorrow never comes too late,
>   And happiness too swiftly flies,

Thought would destroy their paradise.
No more; --where ignorance is bliss,
   'Tis folly to be wise.

Indeed, we can agree with Gray that blissful ignorance is often preferable to painful awareness.

He Hath Disgraced Me

Shylock: He hath disgraced me, and hindered me half a million, laughed at my losses, mocked at my gains, scorned my nation, thwarted my bargains, cooled my friends, heated mine enemies. And what's his reason? I am a Jew. Hath not a Jew eyes? Hath not a Jew hands, organs, dimensions, senses, affections, passions? Fed with the same food, hurt with the same weapons, subject to the same diseases, healed by the same means, warmed and cooled by the same winter and summer as a Christian is? *If you prick us, do we not bleed?* (emphasis mine) (*The Merchant of Venice* 3. 1. 56-68)

PARAPHRASE

Shylock: He has embarrassed me and prevented me from making half a million. He laughed at my losses, mocked my successes, scorned my people, blocked my profits, and caused my friends to lose interest in me, while he encouraged my enemies to rise up against me. And why does he do these things? Because I am a Jew. Doesn't a Jew have eyes? Doesn't a Jew have hands, organs, proportionate body parts, senses, affections, emotions? Isn't a Jew fed with the same food, hurt with the same weapons, vulnerable to the same diseases, healed by the same means, warmed and cooled by the same winter and summer as a Christian? If you prick us, don't we bleed?

*****NOTE:** In the following passage, Aaron the black lover of the Roman Empress Tamora is outraged at the fact that Tamora and her two adult sons have condemned Tamora's infant son to death simply because he is black. They call him "dark," " dismal," "ugly," " a toad." However, just as Tamora's sons are about to kill the child (who is Aaron's son), Aaron rescues him and rebukes them harshly. He then proudly asserts (in essence) the same sentiment that became a popular slogan several centuries later in 1960's America: "Black is beautiful:"

Stay, Murderous Villains! Will You Kill Your Brother?

Aaron: Stay, murderous villains! Will you kill your brother?
....

What, what, ye sanguine, shallow-hearted boys!
Ye white-limed walls! Ye alehouse painted signs!
Coal-black is better than another hue
In that it scorns to bear another hue;
For all the water in the ocean
Can never turn the swan's black legs to white,

> Although she lave them hourly in the flood.
> Tell the Empress from me, I am of age
> To keep mine own—excuse it how she can.
> (*Titus Andronicus* 4. 2. 88; 97-105)

PARAPHRASE

Aaron: Wait, you murderers! You scoundrels! Are you going to kill your own brother? You cowardly, heartless, lily-livered boys! You poor excuses for men! Jet black is better than any other color, since black does not lose its intrinsic strength or integrity even when mixed with another color. For example, all the water in the ocean cannot turn the black legs of the swan to white even if the swan were to wash her legs every hour in the tidal flow. Take this message to the Empress for me. Tell her I am man enough to keep my offspring. She can deny its existence in whatever way she deems fit.

COMMENTARY: A Pricking and Bleeding in New York

"Veni!" Vidi! Vici!" (I came! I saw! I conquered!) was Julius Caesar's victorious utterance. Here is my statement of triumph: I was pricked! I bled! But I overcame!

My first encounter with racism came many years ago when I was in graduate school in New York. While I was an Honors Student at Howard University, I was granted a scholarship to pursue the Ph.D. degree at a leading university in New York. I soon discovered that one of my professors at this university was determined to teach me a lesson: that young black females should not aspire to the Ph. D. degree. From my very first appointment with this man—the day I introduced myself and told him that I was enrolled in his department in pursuit of the doctorate degree—he informed me that as head of the department, he would like to "keep his department small." These were his exact words. He was not even subtle in the message he wished to send me. Instantly, I recognized with incredulity that this man wished to close the door in my face before I even entered, before he even knew me. However, I moved forward unperturbed, hoping that I might have misunderstood the significance of his words.

I didn't have long to wait before I realized that my interpretation was correct. When classes started, I discovered that he was the professor for a number of classes in my curriculum. I was the only black student in all of my classes at this university. Though I excelled in his classes, proving to be most knowledgeable, often being one of the only two students conversant with the material covered, I saw this professor actually agonize that he could not award me a "D" or an "F".

Because of my outstanding performance, this professor (Let's call him Professor X) was constrained to give me an A in one or two of his classes, but he went out of his way to tell me that my A's were "not as good" (his exact words) as the A's he had awarded the white male student who had also demonstrated a good grasp of the class material.

Practically everyday as he lectured, he made some snide remark about the black race, perhaps in an all-out effort to demean me and derail me from achieving my academic goal. For example, one day in class, Professor X digressed and said the following in a mocking tone:

> There is a race of people in the United States who make it difficult for others to know what to call them. If you call them 'Negro' some of them

are offended. If you call them 'colored' some of them are offended. If you call them 'black' some of them are offended. I get around it by referring to all of them as 'people of African descent.' Ha! Ha! Ha!

He then laughed derisively. Bear in mind, I was the only black person in that room, one of approximately twenty-five students. As I looked around the room that evening, I noticed the looks of embarrassment on the faces of the other students. I was encouraged to see that not one of them shared his laughter. Instead, they obviously shared my discomfiture. I found myself helpless in dealing with this problem. Obviously, confrontation is what he wanted so that he could have had an excuse to undermine my grades and force me to withdraw. But I was determined not to let him win.

One evening, near the end of his lecture, he hurriedly put his notes together and announced to the class that he must rush home to watch what he deemed his "favorite television show: 'All in the Family.'" Imagine that! This situation comedy is a humorous satire in which the most notorious bigot, Archie Bunker, denigrates people of all races and ethnicity except white people, targeting black people in particular. It is a successful, enjoyable comedy because it turns on the irony that the ignorant, uninformed, Mr. Malaprop—Archie—considers himself superior to great intellectuals and achievers as long as they are not white.

However, what is sad is the fact that a university professor, a man of letters, selected a trivial, inconsequential, light comedy show to be his most important show on television. I recognized immediately that in embracing Archie Bunker, this bigoted professor could mouth vicariously his derogatory, prejudicial feelings through Archie's foolish rants. I saw exactly what was happening here. You see, Archie Bunker had comedic, artistic, satiric license to say what Professor X wanted to say but could not. That's why Archie was his hero.

I can supply several other examples of the bigotry I encountered in that department, but one or two more will suffice. Eventually, this professor decided to give me a failing grade on a very important exam I had submitted to him. On the pages of my exam paper, I had written extensively on the subject at hand, and I had turned in well-thought-out, well-developed, substantial work on topics I knew very well. Imagine, then, my surprise when Professor X informed me later that I had failed the exam.

Naturally, I protested loudly saying, "Impossible! How could I have failed after supplying so much information?" I demanded an answer. Here is the answer Professor X gave me in response to that question: *"Well, maybe you gave too much information."* Then that man was bold enough to add this statement to the foregoing: *"The Ph.D. is not for everyone"* (his exact words). Ever felt alone and helpless? If yes, then you know how I felt. In other words, he had finally voiced his objection: I have a Ph.D. How dare you seek to be as qualified as I, he was saying in essence.

What could I have done? I had no recourse but to present my case to the dean of the department, citing the clear instances of prejudice and discrimination. I'll never forget that the dean calmly and resolutely informed me that I cannot prove my charges of prejudice and discrimination. Crestfallen, but resolved, I left his office that day, determined to overcome at all cost.

By the way, one last example of the trials I endured at that university will suffice. One day, another professor in the same department returned a paper to me. Let's call him Professor Y. The grade on the paper was a "B". I recall his words to me as he handed me the paper: "Delpha, this paper is worthy of an 'A', but I gave you a 'B' to keep you humble" (his exact words). Imagine that! What an outrage!

And how unwarranted! Actually, I was Humility personified. How much more humility did he want? Therefore, let me paraphrase his words, *You are a young black woman. I gave you a 'B' to keep you in your place.* Oh yes, I was "pricked", and I "bled" in New York, but through unrelenting struggle, and with God's help, I overcame.

20. ALCOHOL ABUSE

INTRODUCTION

Imagine you are on top of the world—literally. You have been on the longest boat ride in history—a cruise that lasted over three hundred days. And now, your boat is resting securely on the top of a mountain somewhere. You have just survived the most colossal deluge, an all-consuming tsunami on this earth. What earth? Actually, it's a new earth, and you and your family are the sole survivors. All other humans have been destroyed. What is so special about me that I have been spared, you ask yourself. There is the potential for your ego to become inflated; however, instead, you are humbled when you stop to think that God has chosen you to be the father of an entirely new earthly population.

Obviously, I make reference to the familiar story of Noah (*Genesis* chapters six, seven, eight, and nine). It is said that Noah "found grace in the eyes of the Lord" (*Genesis* 6:8). God said to Noah, "Come thou and all thy house into the ark; for thee have I seen righteous before me. . . ." (*Genesis* 7:1). The question arises: How could a man of such distinction—a man of such an upright, lofty character—allow himself to be reduced so fully by alcohol? It was as if Lucifer said of Noah: "He thinks he's so special! I know how to get him. Though all else has failed, alcohol will do the trick."

Yes, the Noah incident is one of the most poignant examples of the fact that alcohol can reduce, transform, and destroy greatness in a flash, for shortly after his great victory in escaping the annihilating flood, Noah imbibed to excess and lay naked in a drunken stupor. Two of his sons were so embarrassed by their father's condition that they hastened to cover him without looking at him. But his son and grandson—Ham and Canaan, respectively—are said to have laughed at Noah as he lay in that deplorable condition. Unfortunately, when his sobriety returned, his rebuke or curse of his son and grandson could not erase the stigma.

We can readily agree with the writers who have inveighed against drunkenness so effectively in the following words:

> All excess is ill, but drunkenness is of the worst sort. It spoils health, dismounts the mind, and unmans men. It reveals secrets, is quarrelsome, lascivious, impudent, dangerous and bad.
>
> William Penn (1644-1718)

Here are a few additional words of condemnation:

> Drunkenness is temporary suicide: the happiness that it brings is merely negative, a momentary cessation of unhappiness.
> Bertrand Russell (1872-1970)

The death and destruction, the havoc wreaked by alcohol abuse daily across our nation and in many other parts of the world is common knowledge to us all. William Penn and Bertrand Russell have succinctly summed up the baneful effects of alcohol abuse in the above quotations. At this time, there is no need to rehearse the plethora of ills that surface in the wake of alcohol abuse. However, a word must be said about drunk driving because it is so widespread. It is often associated with sudden death that engulfs the innocent as well as the guilty.

Not long ago, in high day time, a young woman driving drunk somewhere in Florida, killed herself and five young children as well as the occupants of the vehicle with which she collided. Each day, somewhere across our nation, this unfortunate, unnecessary loss of life occurs. We have heard of MADD (Mothers Against Drunk Drivers) and SADD (Students Against Drunk Drivers). Well, I have composed a new acronym: CADD. Here are all the words that the "C" can represent:

The *Community* Against Drunk Drivers

The *Country* Against Drunk Drivers

The *Continent* Against Drunk Drivers

The *Cosmos* Against Drunk Drivers

In other words, all living things are against drunk drivers. If we were to drop the second "D" in "CADD", we would be left with "CAD." Drunk drivers—male or female—are "Cads" indeed: irresponsible, reckless, selfish human beings.

In the two passages that follow, Shakespeare captures expertly the dehumanizing effects of alcohol abuse. He is lamenting the fact that it destroys mind (memory) as well as body.

I Remember a Mass of Things, but Nothing Distinctly

I remember a mass of things, but nothing distinctly—a quarrel, but nothing wherefore. Oh God, that men should put an enemy in their mouths to steal away their brains! That we should, with joy, pleasance, revel, and applause, transform ourselves into beasts!
      (*Othello* 2. 3. 289-94)

PARAPHRASE

I remember many, many things, but I can recall none clearly. I remember a quarrel, but I cannot recall what started it. Dear God, it is hard to understand why men continually put a poisonous substance (an enemy) like alcohol in their mouths even though it damages the brain (alters the mind). It is difficult to understand why, in an atmosphere of gaiety and festivity, with encouragement from others, we often reduce ourselves to the level of beasts.

Though I Cannot Remember What I Did

. . . [T]hough I cannot remember what I did when you made me drunk, yet I am not altogether an ass.
      (*The Merry Wives of Windsor* 1. 1. 174-76)

PARAPHRASE

Although I can't remember what I did when you made me drunk, I am not completely an ass.

COMMENTARY: After Intoxication Comes Transformation

Through the voice of one of his characters, Shakespeare asserts that alcohol is "an enemy" that steals brains and "transform[s]" its victims into "beasts." How apt is this statement! I have seen the destruction, the calamity, the brain stealing, the transformation that inebriation can cause.

Years ago, when I was an undergraduate student at Howard Universty in Washington, D.C., I rented a room in the home of a middle-aged couple. Let's call them Tom and Cynthia Bolton. Most nights, at approximately nine o'clock, Tom's approach would be heralded by his loud, raucous singing heard from a mile away. Cynthia would stand by, on the defensive, ready to right each of Tom's wrongdoings. She seemed to be grateful that Tom's drunkenness did not breed violence as alcohol so often does. No, Tom was not violent, but he was everything else: loud, noisy, sloppy, messy, annoying, argumentative, and uncouth.

When he sat at the table to eat his evening meal, he would push the food around and spill much of it unto the table. After eating and burping, he would take out his dentures and head for the kitchen sink. Cynthia would yell loudly in protest, "No Tom! You mustn't wash your dentures in the kitchen sink. Go upstairs to the bathroom!" However, her words often went unheeded.

Later, most nights, when I was either sleeping or studying in my room, I would hear a knock at my door. When I opened my door, I usually saw Cynthia standing there with an exasperated and embarrassed look on her face.

She would then proceed to ask her usual favor of me: "Tom fell out of the bed. Please come and help me to lift him and get him back in bed." Without a verbal response, I would square my shoulders and march off to the rescue.

Needless to say, my stay at that address was brief. Shakespeare's metaphor or personification of alcohol as a marauding, brain-stealing "enemy" could hardly have been more effectively portrayed than it was in the home of Tom and Cynthia Bolton.

21. PARENT/CHILD CONFLICT

INTRODUCTION

Parent/child conflict is as old as the earth itself. It surfaced in the antediluvian as well as the postdiluvian world. In other words, even before Noah's time, when Cain killed his brother Abel, naturally his parents (Adam and Eve) didn't embrace and applaud him. It simply goes without saying that that first murder must have evoked major conflict between Cain and his parents. Consequently, after God cursed Cain, he became an outcast—a fugitive and a wanderer. And what about Noah's anger and the conflict in his household after his drunken episode? It is said that he cursed his son (Ham) and his grandson (Canaan) with devastating consequences.

Few parent/child conflicts can compare with the classic, familial holocaust that existed in the household of the great King David. Absalom's rebellion against his father brought massive death and destruction in its wake, embroiling an entire nation in civil warfare, as Absalom tried to kill his father and occupy his throne. The conflict between David and Absalom was so pervasive that its retelling spans seven chapters in the Bible (II *Samuel* 13-19), ending with a pitiful scene that tugs at our heartstrings. We hear the loud moans and laments of King David, "O Absalom, my son, my son," and we see a broken, bereaved father whose love for his son far outweighed his son's "sins" against him. Quite possibly, as we watch the weeping David, our eyes moisten and we think of another Father who never stops loving us no matter how much we sin against Him.

Yes, parent/child conflict is cosmic in its reach. It is certainly prevalent on planet earth. Feuds and crises involving children and their parents are among the most recurrent themes and situations presented on popular daily shows like *The Dr. Phil Show, The Judge Judy Show,* and *The Oprah Show.* How often do we hear a daughter or a son say these words to a mother or father: "I want to have nothing more to do with you. You will never see your grandchildren again." Almost daily, we watch the shared agony of children and parents who cannot get along for one reason or another. We also often witness the unfortunate cases of children suing parents and vice versa. In the world of fame and fortune, in Hollywood, for example, we often hear of parents and children who have not spoken to one another for many years because of ongoing feuding.

Conflict involving children and parents is, therefore, one of the seminal problems in our world. What's more, parent/child conflict even permeates the world of make believe and is the cause of turmoil in children's classics and fairytales like "Hansel and Gretel," "Cinderella," and "Snow White and the Seven Dwarfs." The women tormenting the children in these stories are step parents but parents nonetheless. Many of Shakespeare's plays also involve major conflict between parents and children, often leading to dire consequences. The most famous parent/child conflict with deadly consequences exists in the Montague and Capulet households, with Romeo and Juliet respectively as victims. And what about the bitter conflict that arises between members of the royal family in Denmark, as Hamlet condemns his mother and seeks to kill his uncle/step father? So many, many corpses litter the stage at the end of each presentation of *Hamlet*, primarily because of parent/child conflict. The two passages that follow will suffice to demonstrate the acerbity that often exists between parents and their children.

She Is Peevish, Sullen, Froward, Proud, Disobedient

                She is peevish, sullen, forward,
Proud, disobedient, stubborn, lacking duty
Neither regarding that she is my child,
Nor fearing me as if I were her father.
And, may I say to thee, this pride of hers
Upon advice, hath drawn my love from her;
And, where I thought the remnant of mine age
Should have been cherished by her childlike duty,
I now am full resolved to take a wife,
And turn her out to who will take her in.
Then let her beauty be her wedding dower.
For me and my possessions she esteems not.
     (*The Two Gentlemen of Verona* 3. 1. 68-78)

PARAPHRASE

She is disagreeable, sulky, obstinate, proud, disobedient, stubborn, wayward, and headstrong. She disregards the fact that she is my child and denies me the respect I am due as her father. And I might add that experiencing her proud, contrary ways has caused me to withdraw my love from her. Previously, I thought that my old age would have been blessed or enriched by the care and attention a child gives to his or her father. However, I am now quite determined to get married and turn my daughter out of my house. Anyone who wants to take her in is welcome to her, and her beauty can be her dowry, since she appreciates neither me nor my possessions.

Hear, Nature, Hear, Dear Goddess, Hear!

Hear, Nature, hear, dear goddess, hear!
Suspend thy purpose if thou didst intend
To make this creature fruitful.
Into her womb convey sterility.
Dry up in her the organs of increase,
And from her derogate body never spring
A babe to honor her! If she must teem,
Create her child of spleen, that it may live
And be a thwart disnatured torment to her.
Let it stamp wrinkles in her brow of youth,
With cadent tears fret channels in her cheeks,
Turn all her mother's pains and benefits
To laughter and contempt, that she may feel
How sharper than a serpent's tooth it is
To have a thankless child!
   (*King Lear* 1. 4. 297-311)

PARAPHRASE

Mother Nature, please listen to me! Cancel your plans if you intend to make this creature conceive children one day. Make her womb sterile. Dry up or destroy her childbearing organs, and do not allow even one child to issue from her debased body in order to honor her. If she must conceive, let her have a wicked, malicious child who will be a harrowing torment to her for the rest of her life, causing wrinkles to form on her youthful brow. Let her tears flow freely, forming deep furrows in her cheeks. Make a mockery of the pains and blessings surrounding childbearing so that she may discover that it is far more painful for a parent to suffer the sting of a child's ingratitude than for him or her to be bitten by a deadly serpent.

COMMENTARY: Sharper than a Serpent's Tooth and More Deadly

If the question were asked, What are the three most overused and abused words in the English language, I believe that "*I love you*" would head the list. These three magic words are used so often to manipulate, to deceive, to get a desired goal. Too many innocent young girls have gone astray because they heard these words, not being able to recognize feigned love as opposed to true love. It is bad enough when young people are misled. However, it is unfortunate to see older people become victims, caught in the feigned "I love you" trap. This is precisely what happens to Shakespeare's King Lear, and that is why he pronounces such a terrible curse on his daughter Goneril in the preceding passage.

We humans seem to come into this world with an inherent need to be loved. Quite often, it is this need for acceptance that impels some parents to spoil their children and do foolish things. Consider the case of an old, retired father who shares his home with his adult, alcoholic daughter who refuses to work. Although his income is fixed and limited, the father gives his healthy, adult daughter food, clothes, and other needs and wants, even spending money, seeking nothing in return.

So what triggers this sometimes irrational need to be needed? What undergirds our intrinsic quest for approval? Whatever the reason, we humans hunger to hear the words, "I love you," though these words are the undoing of many.

Shakespeare's King Lear is a pivotal example of the tragedy often caused by our hungering and thirsting to hear, "I love you." The Lear plot demonstrates that even a great king can be duped, as young people often are, by an empty profession of love. It is said that Shakespeare borrowed the plot from an incident involving a real King Leir who ruled England around 800 B.C. In his senior years, Leir divided his kingdom between two of his daughters and disinherited his youngest daughter because she did not adequately profess love for him. She then left England and married the King of France. After some time, Leir was abused by his two daughters whom he had made rulers of his kingdom. He then traveled to France, united with the daughter he once rejected, and regained his throne by military force.

Shakespeare's Lear is not as fortunate as the original Leir. In Shakespeare's play, King Lear of England decides to spend his senior years in leisure. His plan is to retire and live, for specified periods, at the homes of his three daughters: Goneril, Regan, and Cordelia. He calls for a map of England, declaring that he intends to divide his kingdom into three parts. He then asks each of his daughters to tell him how much she loves him.

Recognizing that the largest inheritance will most likely fall to the one who professes the greatest love, the oldest daughter Goneril says that her father has all of her love forever. Regan hastens to compete with Goneril, also proclaiming that all of her undying love belongs to her father. Lear is gratified and then turns to his youngest, his favorite, Cordelia expecting to hear an even more exuberant confession of love. However, the honest Cordelia tells him that she loves him as much as she should love a father, but she cannot give him ALL her love, for she must save some for her husband. Lear is furious. He disinherits Cordelia and divides his kingdom between his two older daughters. Needless to say, in less than no time, the insincerity of Goneril and Regan surface, and Lear ends up a tragic figure—homeless, practically friendless, and ravaged by madness. Ironically, it is the rejected Cordelia who rescues him, but both Lear and Cordelia die by the end of the play.

Some parent/child conflicts are, indeed, sharper than a serpent's tooth and more deadly. In homes across America, some clashes involving parents and their children escalate beyond words and actually become deadly. I can recall that very sad day in April, 1984, when the announcement was made on the television and in the newspapers that Marvin Gaye was shot to death by his father. The question that rushed to my mind then, and persists to today, is—What could have gone so terribly wrong to bring about such a deadly consequence? This young, talented artist affectionately labeled the "Prince of Motown" was gone in a flash.

Another incident, even more mind-boggling, took place a few weeks ago somewhere in Florida. Even as I read the information in the newspaper and heard it on television, it was still difficult for me to visualize or comprehend. Imagine that a mother killed her two children—a boy and a girl—because, she claimed, they talked back to her. According to the newscast, this is how the incident unfolded. She was driving her son (around thirteen years old) to a sports activity. He must have said something to annoy her, so she killed him on the street. She then turned the vehicle around, with her dead son inside, and headed back home where she found her eleven-year-old daughter sitting at her computer, doing her homework. Without hesitating, without compunction, she killed her also. Unbelievable!

And what about the teenager (also in Florida) who killed both of his parents with a hammer, a few months ago, and held a large party that same night in their home, while the blood-soaked bodies of his parents lay in their bedroom? There are some occurrences in this life that defy explanation and challenge comprehension.

22. THE SUPERNATURAL—SUPERSTITION—THE WORLD OF THE OCCULT

INTRODUCTION

Thousands of years ago, King Saul—the first king of Israel—went to a medium in desperation. Through this medium, the Witch of Endor, he sought to make contact with the spirit world so that he could gain advice from the highly respected but deceased prophet Samuel (I *Samuel* 28: 7-25). The woman conjured up an apparition that appeared to be Samuel.

Believe it or not, today mediums are sought out as much as they ever were. People are paying large sums to be able to communicate with deceased relatives or acquaintances. Just the other day, a famous medium was featured on one of the most popular daytime television shows. Surely enough, he picked people "at random" in the audience and left television and home audiences stunned and in awe when he told these people the names of their dead relatives and delivered messages—including familial information—allegedly from the dead. Remember, he had never seen the people in the television audience before.

Nonsense, I hear some of my readers saying. That had to be a fake performance in which he pretended not to know those people, some may argue. However, I crave your indulgence for a moment. I ask kindly for a willing suspension of your disbelief and beg you to read on to the end of this chapter. By then, I will have presented a logical explanation for the existence of mediums, ghosts, apparitions, obeah, necromancy and the like. I will also put the spotlight on the evil agent behind all the mayhem in the occult world.

Speaking of mediums, I am about to relate an incident which is factual. It happened to my mother many years ago in Montserrat, West Indies. She had a strange encounter. One day, she decided to buy some bricks and build an oven in our backyard so that she could bake some bread for us. She placed brick upon brick until the oven was built. She then stepped back proudly to examine her handiwork when, Crash! The oven suddenly collapsed. All the bricks fell to the ground. Exhausted and disappointed, she retraced her steps, picked up each brick, piled it atop another, and arranged them carefully until the oven was nicely built once more. But shortly thereafter, for no apparent reason, the bricks fell once more in a disheveled heap.

As she collected the bricks for the third time—frustrated, exasperated, and bewildered—a young woman, known to be a medium, approached her and said, "Mrs. B, I feel so sorry for you. You are not going to be able to build that oven today. Each time you complete it, Thomas deliberately pushes all of the bricks to the ground." Who was Thomas, you might ask. Thomas was a young man who had died and was buried two days earlier. The medium continued, "He is standing right there, not too far from you. He is waiting to push the bricks down again the moment you rebuild the oven. I can see him, but you can't." Some may still remain shrouded in disbelief even after hearing stories like the one I just related. However, this and similar occurrences were not only real but also prevalent during the early days in Montserrat and Antigua, the days before electricity—the days I call the "period of darkness."

My mother and father have had their own supernatural experiences with poltergeists and various other forms of manifestations. I could write a book about the many hair-raising episodes in the lives of people my mother and father knew well during the period of darkness. My siblings and I were terrified, but at the same time fascinated, as we listened to the "ghost" stories our parents told us. We heard about a headless donkey walking around in the dark. We heard of a rider-less horse that materialized at night from nowhere and galloped at full speed towards two petrified, defenseless sisters and then disappeared.

We also listened intently as they told us about a preacher who was all alone in a large building. He came home one night and became seriously ill as soon as he opened the door to his bedroom. He sensed a presence in his bedroom, but saw nothing. He then reached for his Bible and began to read from the Psalms. Shortly thereafter, he heard high-heeled, female footsteps leading from his bed heading towards the closed door. He then listened as the footsteps passed outside his window, and he heard each receding click,

click, click of the high-heeled shoes progress down the long, cemented corridor until the footsteps were heard no more. Remember, the door of his bedroom was still closed. After the footsteps died, strangely enough, the preacher suddenly felt better. The life that seemed to have been ebbing from his body was fully restored. To this day, he still speaks of that disturbing experience.

However, of all the incidents, none is as scary as one our parents told us about a funeral procession on a road in Montserrat at midnight. On the night that we heard about this encounter, my siblings and I slept in one room, for not one of us was brave enough to sleep alone that night.

When supernatural incidents like the ones I have recounted occur, it is unfortunate that many of the people involved do not recognize that the devil has the power to deceive and wreak havoc in our lives. The Bible speaks of the "wiles of the devil" and reminds us that "we wrestle not against flesh and blood, but against principalities, . . . against the rulers of the darkness of this world. . . ." (*Ephesians* 6: 12). It is sad that so many people who believe in ghosts, spirits, voices, and apparitions from the grave do not recognize that the dead know nothing and cannot communicate with anyone or do anything whether good or bad.

Yes, there have been apparitions and manifestations and, yes, so-called ghosts in our contemporary world, as well as before that—in Shakespeare's world, and long before that—in the ancient world. However, regardless of the location, these supernatural occurrences are the handiwork of the devil who impersonates the dead in order to mislead and confuse the living. Obviously, centuries ago, Shakespeare recognized the possibility that the devil was behind these machinations. And what about superstition? Those who avoid every crack so as not to break their mothers' backs, and those who become terrified when a black cat crosses their paths are needlessly succumbing to superstition and, unfortunately, are living from day to day imprisoned by their unwarranted fears.

Shakespeare's plays are replete with references and incidents involving the occult. In major plays like *Hamlet*, *Macbeth*, and *Julius Caesar*, ghosts have an almost equal impact on the plots as do the major characters. For example, the ghost of Hamlet's father broods over and dominates the entire plot of *Hamlet.*. Macbeth's encounter with the three witches (at the very beginning of *Macbeth*) triggers the major action surrounding Macbeth's rise and fall, and Caesar's death is heralded in the medium/soothsayer's warning, "Beware the Ides of March!" The episodes in the excerpts that follow are just a few selected from the many supernatural and superstitious references and occurrences in Shakespeare's plays.

Sir, Your Queen Must Overboard

First Sailor: Sir, your Queen must overboard. The sea works high, the wind is loud, and will not lie till the ship be cleared of the dead.

Pericles: That's your superstition.

First Sailor: Pardon us, sir. With us at sea it hath been still observed, and we are strong in custom. Therefore briefly yield her, for she must overboard straight.
      (*Pericles* III. 1. 47-54)

PARAPHRASE

First Sailor: Sir, your queen must be thrown overboard. Huge waves are stirred up, and the wind howls fiercely. The storm that rages will not

	be subdued until the corpse is thrown overboard.
Pericles:	You are allowing your superstition to get the better of you.
First Sailor:	Excuse us, sir. But during the many years that we sailors have spent at sea, we have always noticed this reaction in the sea, and we are very serious. Therefore, cast her body overboard without hesitating another minute.

But It Is Doubtful Yet Whether Caesar Will Come Forth

Cassius:
        But it is doubtful yet
Whether Caesar will come forth today or no,
For he is superstitious grown of late,
Quite from the main opinion he held once
Of fantasy, of dreams and ceremonies.
It may be these apparent prodigies,
The unaccustomed terror of this night***
And the persuasion of his augurers,
May hold him from the Capitol today.
      (*Julius Caesar* 2. 1. 193-201)

***NOTE: There was a violent storm the night before Caesar's assassination: howling winds, lightning, thunder, and a deluge.

PARAPHRASE

It is uncertain whether Caesar will come out today, because lately he has become superstitious, contrary to the strong opinion he held previously concerning the connection between ceremonies, dreams, and supernatural events. Perhaps the terrifying signs of disaster that we witnessed in nature—the unusual horror of last night—and the advice of his soothsayers (prophets, mediums) may discourage him from coming to the Capitol today.

Ha! Who Comes Here?

Brutus speaks as he sees the ghost of Caesar:

> Ha! Who comes here?
> I think it is the weakness of mine eyes
> That shapes this monstrous apparition.
> It comes upon me. Art thou anything?
> Art thou some god, some angel, or some devil,
> That makest my blood cold, and my hair to stare?
> Speak to me what thou art.
>   (*Julius Caesar* 4. 3. 275-281)

PARAPHRASE

Ha! Who is this approaching me? I believe that because of the dimness of my eyes I might be seeing this horrendous phantom that isn't actually there. But it is right before me. Are you anything substantial? Tangible? Are you a god, an angel, or a devil? You make my blood run cold and my hair stand on end. Speak to me! Tell me, who or what are you?

Delpha Charles, Ph.D.

Angels and Ministers of Grace Defend Us!

***NOTE:** Hamlet sees the ghost of his father, the deceased king of Denmark, and tries to engage the apparition in conversation.

Angels and ministers of grace defend us!
Be thou a spirit of health or goblin damned,
Bring with thee airs from Heaven or blasts from
    Hell,
Be thy intents wicked or charitable,
Thou comest in such a questionable shape
That I will speak to thee. I'll call thee Hamlet,
King, Father, royal Dane. Oh, answer me!
Let me not burst in ignorance, but tell
Why thy canonized bones, hearsed in death,
Have burst their cerements, why the sepulcher
Wherein we saw thee quietly inurned
Hath oped his ponderous and marble jaws
To cast thee up again. What may this mean,
That thou, dead corse, again, in complete steel,
Revisit'st thus the glimpses of the moon,
Making night hideous, and we fools of nature
So horridly to shake our disposition
With thoughts beyond the reaches of our souls?
Say, why is this? Wherefore? What should we do?
    (*Hamlet* 1. 4. 39-57)

PARAPHRASE

Angels and ministering spirits protect us! Are you an ethereal spirit or one condemned to hell? Do you bring blessings from heaven or damnation from hell? Are your intentions evil or good? You come in such a mysterious shape that I will speak to you; I'll call you Hamlet, King, father, royal Dane. Please answer me. Don't let me be consumed by ignorance! Tell me why your bones, duly buried in the sanctity of the church, and now shrouded in death, have ripped open the winding sheet that confined them. Why has the tomb where we saw you peacefully interred opened its vast jaws to eject you again? What does this mean? What is the explanation for the fact that you—a corpse clothed in complete armor—walk once again in the moonlight, making the night hideous (ominous) and stirring our emotions to such an extent that unfathomable, inexplicable thoughts crowd our minds, especially because we are unskilled in the art of interpreting the mysteries of life. Speak! Tell us why you have appeared! What does your presence mean? What would you have us do?

COMMENTARY: The Mysterious Hand and Bugs from The Unknown

Oh yes! The devil has been busy and has sought to assault the human intellect and faith in God with his evil machinations. I could, indeed, write a book about supernatural events that were prevalent in the early days in Montserrat and Antigua. It would be a hair-raising book. I would give Washington Irving (1783-1859) a run for his money in this book which I could possibly title *Legends of Two Sleepy Islands* (similar to Irving's "The Legend of Sleepy Hollow"). However, the main difference between Irving's work and mine (if I were to undertake this project) is the fact that Irving's stories were "legend." Mine would be factual accounts of incidents in the lives of people who actually lived in Montserrat and Antigua during the early days. For example, the two stories that follow are no "legend." These were supernatural encounters in the lives of real people, and I was an eye witness to both of them.

Travel back with me several decades to a tumultuous day in the city of St. John's, Antigua. There is inexpressible terror in the streets. People are rushing about, practically in circular motion, neither going forward nor backward, but simply asking the same questions repeatedly, "Did you see her? Did you hear it? Others are querying just as insistently, "See whom? Hear what?" I am one of those people who struggle to gain coherence from incoherence.

Eventually, I manage to hear that a young woman (let's call her Emma) is being beaten practically to death before the eyes of all onlookers. She is knocked to the ground in front of her home, and the blows fall heavily on her twisted face in rapid succession. But here's the part that defies belief. Her attacker is invisible. What! I know my readers are inclined to exclaim. However, the event I am relating took place in broad daylight before many eye witnesses, people who had rushed to Emma's house to see the incredible spectacle for themselves. Others kept advancing one pace and retreating two, too scared to go near Emma's house in case an invader from Mars or some nether region intended to destroy all mortals one by one. In any case, let me take my readers back to the scene and make them eye witnesses as the events unfolded.

Picture Emma lying, writhing on the ground. Her face is swollen. The large masculine hand has left an oversized palm print etched in red across her face. She cringes, squirms, and whimpers in anticipation of the next slap that is about to ravage her face. She tries to cover her face with her hands, to no avail. Pow! Pow! Pow! Again and again, this is what onlookers hear, as some demonic, unseen hand connects to the young woman's face repeatedly. She shrieks in agony.

Someone says, "Let's get her into the house. But there is some hesitancy. And why not! The onlookers are afraid that in touching Emma or helping her in any way, they may incur the wrath of the supernatural attacker and direct his vengeance towards them and their children. However, some brave soul comes forward and carries Emma inside to her bed. Many in the crowd follow, and someone suggests that all the doors and windows should be locked, hoping that Emma would now be protected from whoever or whatever was attacking her outside. That being accomplished, they wait in silence. But the wait is brief. Suddenly, a loud slap violates the silence in the room and reverberates against the walls while the terrified people in the room make a mad dash for the door.

Emma has collapsed on the floor, and preparation is being made to transport her to the hospital. When she arrives at the hospital, all of the nurses leave their stations and rush to her bedside in consternation, incredulity, and curiosity. However, they too stand by helplessly and listen to the loud slaps and see the large welts and huge, red palm print on Emma's swollen face.

A young and up-coming calypsonian in Antigua gained fame and island acclaim because he wrote a calypso to mark this supernatural incident: "The slapping hand slaps again!" He sang. His voice reached his immediate audience and traveled from the stage to the farthest reaches of the Caribbean. Emma's strange encounter was also documented in many Caribbean newspapers. Curious people rushed from Montserrat, St. Kitts, Nevis, Dominica, Jamaica, Trinidad, Barbados, Guadeloupe, and other Caribbean islands to see this inexplicable supernatural phenomenon. I have no idea whether Emma survived after this harrowing experience. The slapping hand remains a mystery to this day.

Similar mysteries, thought to be the result of obeah or necromancy, also occurred in other Caribbean islands during the early years. One additional example will suffice. Everybody in the Melas Village knew about the army of unnatural, menacing bed bugs—from some nether region—that invaded the home of the Brent family and took up residence in all areas of their home: in the bedrooms, the living room, the kitchen, the closets, in the family's clothes, and in the hair of all the Brent children. Even as they sat in school, the Brents were humiliated as the sinister bugs paraded about in their hair, on their necks, and on their clothing.

Actually, the Brent family was one of the most outstanding, upper class, and respectable families not only in the Melas Village but also in the entire island. Imagine, therefore, the chatter, the tongue wagging, the whispers, the ridicule, the stares, and the gossip as the Melasians witnessed the spectacle of the proliferating bugs that were seen in the hair of even the babies in the family.

The hair of the Brent family members was washed almost daily, and hot combs were applied. But the hot combs destroyed the hair instead of the bugs. The Brents' clothing was clean, and the house scrubbed and swept frequently. However, the more impeccable the home and its occupants were, the more the bugs multiplied. Many prayers and lamentations were uttered daily but to no avail. A preacher was called in to re-bless the house, to no avail.

This calamity was the consequence of the green-eyed monster: jealousy which is a nasty complaint. It can be a deadly emotion. Ironically, the colloquial expression "lousy" forms the major part of this word. It is "lousy" indeed to hate others or wish them harm just because they are more successful, more accomplished, or more endowed. Covetousness is a sin, the Bible reminds us. And yet, with its counterpart, jealousy, it is a cancer that can imperceptibly destroy families and whole communities.

Jealousy can cause murders and social tsunamis. It was jealousy that triggered the very first murder when Cain killed his brother Abel (*Genesis* chapter 4). It was jealousy that violated Jacob's senior years when his envious sons sold his favorite child, Joseph, to slavery and told Jacob that Joseph was dead (*Genesis* chapter 37). It was jealousy that made David a relentlessly hunted fugitive, for many years, pursued by the vengeful Saul (1 *Samuel* 17-24).

Approximately six months before the onslaught of bugs in the Brent home, Cynthia Banter, an evil troll of a woman, made no effort to hide the fact that she hated Mrs. Brent and her family. She often said to her friends, "They think that they are better than the rest of us. Their house is always clean and attractive, and Mrs. Brent is too proud of her children." Cynthia Banter was known to be a dealer in necromancy. One day, she picked a fight with Mrs. Brent and threw these spiteful words at her: "From the day your children are born on this earth, they will have bugs in their hair and everywhere."

When we hear of or witness supernatural incidents like the ones described in this chapter, we are incredulous, and we wonder how are they possible. But doubt does not linger when we recall St. Paul's words:

> For we wrestle not against flesh and blood,
> but against principalities, against powers,
> against the rulers of the darkness of this
> world, against spiritual wickedness in high
> places. (*Ephesians* 6: 12)

St. Paul reminds us that though we are physically weaker than the powers of darkness that surround us, we have within our reach the "whole armour of God" to fortify us and empower us to "stand against the wiles of the devil." In a flash, we can stand protected from head to foot, poised for warfare, like Roman soldiers with their helmets, their breastplates, their swords, and their shields:

> Stand therefore, having your loins girt about
> with truth, and having on the breastplate of
> righteousness; And your feet shod with the
> preparation of the gospel of peace; Above all,
> taking the shield of faith, wherewith ye shall
> be able to quench all the fiery darts of the wicked.
> And take the helmet of salvation, and the sword

of the Spirit, which is the word of God: Praying always with all prayer and supplication in the Spirit. . . .
(*Ephesians* 6: 14-18)

With this invincible, God-given armament, we are empowered and equipped to conquer all foes, demonic or otherwise, and we shall be able to exclaim victoriously with St. Paul:

I have fought a good fight, I have finished my course, I have kept the faith: Henceforth there is laid up for me a crown of righteousness, which the Lord, the righteous judge, shall give me at that day: and not to me only, but unto all them also that love his appearing.
(2 *Timothy* 4: 7-8)

And I say, "Amen!"